On My Own

PRACTICE WORKBOOK

Harcourt Brace & Company

Orlando • Atlanta • Austin • Boston • San Francisco • Chicago • Dallas • New York • Toronto • London

http://www.hbschool.com

W9-AUF-238

Copyright © by Harcourt Brace & Company

All rights reserved. No part of this publication may be reproduced or transmitted in any form or by any means, electronic or mechanical, including photocopy, recording, or any information storage and retrieval system, without permission in writing from the publisher.

Permission is hereby granted to individual teachers using the corresponding student's textbook or kit as the major vehicle for regular classroom instruction to photocopy complete pages from this publication in classroom quantities for instructional use and not for resale.

Duplication of this work other than by individual classroom teachers under the conditions specified above requires a license. To order a license to duplicate this work in greater than classroom quantities, contact Customer Service, Harcourt Brace & Company, 6277 Sea Harbor Drive, Orlando, Florida 32887-6777. Telephone: 1-800-225-5425. Fax: 1-800-874-6418 or 407-352-3442.

HARCOURT BRACE and Quill Design is a registered trademark of Harcourt Brace & Company. MATH ADVANTAGE is a trademark of Harcourt Brace & Company.

Printed in the United States of America

ISBN 0-15-311045-7

13 14   082   2004 2003 2002

CONTENTS

Using Numbers

Vocabulary

Fill in the blanks.

1. _____ numbers tell how many.

2. _____ numbers tell position or order.

3. _____ numbers name things.

Tell whether each number is expressed as a *cardinal, ordinal,* or *nominal.*

4. The area of Cheryl's room is 130 sq ft.

_____

5. Laura won first place in the dance contest.

_____

6. Frank scored 23 points in a basketball game.

_____

7. Michael Jordan wears the number 23 on his jersey.

_____

8. Mr. Lenny put a teaspoon of sugar in his coffee.

_____

9. Amanda's mother is 39 years old.

_____

Mixed Applications

For Problems 10–12, use the table.

10. What are the total miles walked by the 3 winners?

_____

WALK FOR HEALTH		
Winners	**Name**	**Miles Walked**
1st Place	Juan-Carlos	37
2nd Place	Sarah	34
3rd Place	Frank	32

11. Frank walked at the same speed for 8 hours. How far did he walk in 1 hour?

_____

12. If each mile walked raised $2.25, did Juan-Carlos earn more than or less than $75.00?

_____

Benchmark Numbers

Vocabulary

Fill in the blank.

1. A _____ is a point of reference.

Use the benchmark number to choose the more reasonable estimate.

2.

90 or 900 _____

3.

50 or 500 _____

Write *yes* or *no* to tell whether the estimate is reasonable.

4. • 40 nickels in a roll
   • 8 rolls of nickels
   Estimate: There are about 300 nickels.

   _____

5. • 8 slices per pizza
   • 20 pizzas in the cafeteria
   Estimate: There are about 100 pizza slices in the cafeteria.

   _____

6. • 20 tables in a restaurant
   • Each table seats 6 people.
   Estimate: The restaurant seats about 100 people.

   _____

7. • 10 rolls of film in a case
   • Each roll has 24 exposures.
   Estimate: There are about 100 exposures of film in a case.

   _____

Mixed Applications

8. Each shelf in a store can display about 30 boxes of cards. The store has 11 shelves. About how many boxes of cards can the store display?

   _____

9. Each of 65 students drank a fruit juice for lunch. If the fruit juice comes in six-packs, how many six-packs were needed?

   _____

Place Value to Hundred Thousands

Write the value of the **bold-faced** digit.

1. 251,469

2. 747,322

3. 638,415

_____   _____   _____

_____   _____   _____

Complete.

4. 371,695 = (___ × 100,000) + (___ × 10,000) + (___ × 1,000) + (___ × 100)

+ (___ × 10) + (___ × 1)

5. 279,956 = (___ × 100,000) + (___ × 10,000) + (___ × 1,000) + (___ × 100)

+ (___ × 10) + (___ × 1)

6. 986,741 = (9 × _____) + (8 × _____) + (6 × _____)

+ (7 × _____) + (4 × _____) + (1 × _____)

Write the expanded numbers in standard form.

7. 400,000 + 70,000 + 9,000 + 500 + 60 + 9   _____

8. 100,000 + 90,000 + 0 + 300 + 0 + 1   _____

9. 700,000 + 50,000 + 5,000 + 0 + 40 + 6   _____

10. 600,000 + 80,000 + 3,000 + 0 + 0 + 0   _____

Mixed Applications

11. In 1994, the American Kennel Club registered 132,051 Labrador Retrievers. What is the value of the digit 3 in this number?

_____

_____

12. This year, Connie earned $56,426 as a sales manager. Last year she earned $49,378. How much more did Connie earn this year?

_____

_____

Place Value to Hundred Millions

Write the value of the **bold-faced** digit.

1. 301,**7**24,469

2. 4**2**6,379,831

3. 234,5**6**7,890

_____

_____

_____

_____

_____

_____

4. **1**89,612,357

5. 521,**8**74,394

6. 879,464,978

_____

_____

_____

_____

_____

_____

Write two other forms for each number.

7. 125,740,689 _____

_____

_____

8. 200,403,926 _____

_____

_____

9. 600,000,000 + 0 + 9,000,000 + 700,000 + 60,000 + 0 + 400 + 30 + 1

_____

_____

10. eight hundred ninety-five million, four hundred six thousand, two hundred twenty-five

_____

_____

Mixed Applications

11. The CD-ROM for *Grolier's Multimedia Encyclopedia* holds 638,400,000 bits of information. What is the value of the digit 8 in this number?

12. Every 225 Earth days, the planet Venus travels around the sun an average distance of 67,000,000 miles. Write the distance in word form.

_____

_____

Comparing and Ordering

Write <, >, or = for each ◯ .

1. 532 ◯ 523

2. 6,475 ◯ 6,574

3. 7,821 ◯ 7,821

4. 59,495 ◯ 54,945

Order from greatest to least.

5. 354; 345; 435

6. 7,685; 7,856; 7,568

_____

_____

7. 45,732; 47,325; 42,537

8. 654,837; 675,384; 648,753

_____

_____

Order from least to greatest.

9. 647; 746; 467

10. 6,785; 6,875; 6,587

_____

_____

11. 15,234; 15,423; 15,342

12. 324,987; 432,789; 734,298

_____

_____

Mixed Applications

For Problems 13–16, use the table.

13. Which of these waterfalls is the longest?

_____

14. Which waterfall is longer, Iguacu Falls or Churchill Falls?

_____

15. How much longer is Victoria Falls than Churchill Falls?

_____

Waterfall	Length
Victoria Falls	355 ft
Yellowstone Falls	308 ft
Churchill Falls	250 ft
Iguacu Falls	280 ft

16. Which of these waterfalls is the shortest?

_____

Problem-Solving Strategy

Use a Table

Use a table and solve.

HAWAIIAN ISLANDS	
Island	**Area (square miles)**
Maui	729
Hawai'i	4,038
O'ahu	608
Kaua'i	553

1. This table shows some of the Hawaiian Islands and their areas. Which island has the greatest area? the least area?

_____

CALIFORNIA CITIES	
City	**Population**
San Diego	1,110,549
Los Angeles	3,485,398
Long Beach	429,433
San Francisco	723,959

2. This table shows some of the major cities in California and their populations. Order the cities from largest population to smallest population.

_____

_____

Mixed Applications

Solve.

CHOOSE A STRATEGY

- **Work Backward**   - **Use a Table**   - **Act It Out**   - **Make an Organized List**

3. Romona worked 9 hours over the weekend. She worked twice as many hours on Saturday as on Sunday. How many hours did she work on Saturday? on Sunday?

_____

4. Anna spent half her money on lunch. She spent half her remaining money on a book. She had $2 remaining. How much money did Anna begin with?

_____

5. School T-shirts are available in sizes small, medium, and large. Color choices are blue or red. Make a list of all possible T-shirt choices.

_____

_____

6. Allison is shorter than Pam and taller than Jane. Jane is taller than Ellen. Who is the tallest person?

_____

Adding and Subtracting with Data

Vocabulary

Fill in the blank.

1. Addition and subtraction are _____.
One operation undoes the other operation.

For Exercises 2–4, use the data in the table.

2. How many books were collected in all?

_____

3. How many more books were collected by Ms. Carvajal's class than Mr. Tyse's class?

_____

4. Which two classrooms together collected 159 books?

_____

Sixth-Grade Book Collection	
Mr. Tyse	72 books
Ms. Carvajal	86 books
Mrs. Langway	91 books
Ms. Beebe	81 books
Mrs. Voglino	78 books
Ms. Benfosado	83 books

Write the related number sentence. Find the sum or difference.

5. $71 - 53 = n$

_____

6. $114 - 86 = n$

_____

7. $63 + n = 91$

_____

8. $36 + n = 68$

_____

Mixed Applications

9. Niki scored 36 total points in a basketball game. She scored 12 points in the second half of the game. How many points did Niki score in the first half of the game?

_____

10. Niki's basketball team won 12 games and lost 18 games. How many games did her team play?

_____

More About Subtracting

Draw the counters after regrouping. Find the difference.

1. 635
    − 327

Hundreds	Tens	Ones
○○○ ○○○	○○ ○	○○ ○○ ○

2. 514
    − 227

Hundreds	Tens	Ones
○○○ ○○	○	○○ ○○

Hundreds	Tens	Ones

_____

Hundreds	Tens	Ones

_____

Find the difference. You may use counters.

3. 321
    − 174

4. 476
    − 298

5. 512
    − 251

6. 347
    − 165

7. 722
    − 457

8. 657
    − 278

9. 928
    − 439

10. 845
    − 259

11. 1,452
    − 694

12. 3,425
    − 2,857

13. 5,413
    − 2,336

14. 8,641
    − 3,568

Mixed Applications

For Problems 15–17, use the table.

15. How many more points did Jeff score than Bill?

_____

16. How many more points did Jeff score than Dave?

_____

BASKETBALL LEADING SCORERS	
Name	Points
Jeff	342
Bill	276
Dave	245

17. What is the total number of points scored by Jeff, Bill, and Dave?

_____

18. Nadia bought 5 books that cost $3.99 each. What was the total cost of Nadia's purchase?

_____

Subtracting Across Zeros

Show how you regrouped for each problem. Solve.

1. $\begin{array}{r} 500 \\ -236 \\ \hline \end{array}$

2. $\begin{array}{r} 3{,}000 \\ -1{,}721 \\ \hline \end{array}$

3. $\begin{array}{r} 7{,}003 \\ -4{,}875 \\ \hline \end{array}$

4. $\begin{array}{r} 15{,}000 \\ -11{,}484 \\ \hline \end{array}$

Find the difference.

5. $\begin{array}{r} 400 \\ -265 \\ \hline \end{array}$

6. $\begin{array}{r} 700 \\ -527 \\ \hline \end{array}$

7. $\begin{array}{r} 3{,}000 \\ -782 \\ \hline \end{array}$

8. $\begin{array}{r} 4{,}003 \\ -2{,}726 \\ \hline \end{array}$

9. $\begin{array}{r} 9{,}000 \\ -7{,}623 \\ \hline \end{array}$

10. $\begin{array}{r} 5{,}000 \\ -2{,}966 \\ \hline \end{array}$

11. $\begin{array}{r} 10{,}000 \\ -8{,}329 \\ \hline \end{array}$

12. $\begin{array}{r} 14{,}000 \\ -6{,}451 \\ \hline \end{array}$

13. $\begin{array}{r} 16{,}000 \\ -11{,}469 \\ \hline \end{array}$

14. $\begin{array}{r} 20{,}000 \\ -6{,}817 \\ \hline \end{array}$

15. $\begin{array}{r} 25{,}000 \\ -13{,}475 \\ \hline \end{array}$

16. $\begin{array}{r} 60{,}000 \\ -28{,}937 \\ \hline \end{array}$

Mixed Applications

17. Hillside Elementary School has 625 students. Valley Elementary School has 438 students. How many more students go to Hillside?

_____

18. The Great Western Forum seats 17,505 fans for basketball games. If there are 2,638 empty seats, how many people are at the game?

_____

19. A writer took in $6,001. She paid $2,016 in taxes. How much money did she make?

_____

20. There are 2,000 milliliters in a 2-liter bottle of soda. If you serve five 250 milliliter cups of soda, how many milliliters of soda do you have left?

_____

Choosing Addition or Subtraction

Choose and name the operation. Solve.

1. Mimi collected 246 bottles to recycle. Carlos collected 178 bottles. How many more bottles did Mimi collect?

_____

2. Brett had 428 animal stickers. He received 35 more for his birthday. What is the total number of stickers Brett has?

_____

3. The school raffle committee printed 15,000 raffle tickets. The students sold all but 924. How many tickets did the students sell?

_____

4. George ate a sandwich with 350 calories. He drank a glass of milk with 110 calories. How many total calories did George consume?

_____

5. Gretchen was born in 1990. Her grandfather was born in 1933. How much older than Gretchen is her grandfather?

_____

6. Katrina bought a CD player for $126 and 3 CD's for $29. How much did she spend in all?

_____

Mixed Applications

For Problems 7–10, use the table.

7. Is the total length of the Great Lakes greater than or less than 1,200 miles?

_____

THE GREAT LAKES		
Lake	Length	Maximum Depth
Superior	350 mi	1,330 ft
Michigan	307 mi	923 ft
Erie	241 mi	210 ft
Huron	206 mi	750 ft
Ontario	193 mi	802 ft

8. Lake Erie is the shallowest Great Lake. How much deeper is Lake Superior?

_____

9. The Illinois River is 240 mi long. How much longer is Lake Michigan than the Illinois River?

_____

10. What is the total depth of Lake Erie and Lake Michigan?

_____

Estimation and Column Addition

Vocabulary

Fill in the blank.

1. Numbers that are easy to compute mentally are

_____ .

Choose a method, and then estimate each sum.

2.	17	3.	28	4.	91	5.	18
	26		45		16		74
	34		62		25		69
	+ 42		+ 76		+ 34		+ 86

6.	118	7.	449	8.	751	9.	340
	235		250		832		568
	486		368		244		455
	+ 379		+ 196		+ 628		+ 832

10.	647	11.	191	12.	361	13.	261
	353		157		158		342
	621		438		311		557
	+ 550		+ 571		+ 769		+ 923

Mixed Applications

14. In Mrs. Ryan's class, Mike, Bill, Sharim, and Jo collected cans for recycling. Mike collected 139 cans, Bill—125 cans, Sharim—159 cans, and Jo—246 cans. About how many cans were collected by all four students?

_____

15. In a timed situp test, Mike did 42 situps, Bill did 24 situps, Sharim did 31 situps, and Jo did 48 situps. How many situps did they do in all?

_____

Problem-Solving Strategy

Estimate or Exact Answer?

Decide whether you need to estimate, find the exact answer, or both. Solve.

1. Ben received $10.00 for doing chores. He wants to buy some cards for $2.89, an action figure for $4.99, and a comic book for $1.79. Does he have enough to pay for all three items? How much will Ben pay at the cash register? How much change will he receive?

_____

2. Yasmin received $50.00 for her birthday. She wants to buy a sweater for $13.99, a necklace for $14.95, and shoes for $19.98. Does Yasmin have enough money to pay for all three items? How much will she pay? How much change will she receive?

_____

3. Catherine wants to buy some roses for $6.99, some potting soil for $3.98, and a ceramic pot for $7.95. She has $20.00. How much will she spend on the items? How much change will she receive?

_____

4. Mark has $30.00 to spend on party favors. He wants to buy party horns for $9.95, candy for $5.98, and magic tricks for $15.99. Does Mark have enough money for all three items?

_____

Mixed Applications

Solve.

CHOOSE A STRATEGY

- Use a Table   • Guess and Check   • Write a Number Sentence   • Work Backward

5. Walt bought a CD player on sale for $99.95 plus $4.99 tax. The regular price was $149.99 including tax. How much did Walt save?

_____

6. Emma spent $4 on cards and $18 on a sweater. Emma has $9 left. How much did Emma begin with?

_____

7. In an even 2-digit number, the second digit is 3 times the first. What is the number?

_____

8. Don is a cashier. When he calculates the amount of change, does he want an estimate or the exact answer?

_____

Name _____

Using Tenths and Hundredths

Write the letter of the decimal that matches each model.

1.

2.

3.

_____   _____   _____

a. 2.03   b. 1.22   c. 1.11

Write the decimal for each.

4. eight and thirteen hundredths

_____

5. four and three tenths

_____

6. sixty-five hundredths

_____

7. five and one tenth

_____

8. six and five hundredths

_____

9. seven and twenty-two hundredths

_____

10. 3 + 0.4

_____

11. 5 + 0 + 0.01

_____

12. 7 + 0.9 + 0.03

_____

13. 0.2 + 0.09

_____

14. 4 + 0.5 + 0.02

_____

15. 12 + 0.7 + 0.04

_____

Mixed Applications

16. Sophia ran the 100-meter dash in 11.36 seconds. What is the value of the 3 in her time?

_____

17. Frank ran the 100-meter race in 10.09 seconds. Write Frank's time in written form.

_____

18. One school district raised $12,195 in a town-wide fund raiser. A second school district raised $9,468. How much more money did the first district raise?

_____

19. Gloria's room is 12 feet long and 15 feet wide. What is the area of Gloria's room? the perimeter?

_____

_____

Thousandths

Vocabulary

Fill in the blank.

1. One milliliter equals one _____ of a liter.

Use base-ten blocks to model each number. Record the number in a place-value chart.

2. 6.254

Ones	Tenths	Hundredths	Thousandths

3. 9.064

Ones	Tenths	Hundredths	Thousandths

Write in standard form.

4. six thousandths

_____

5. sixty-eight thousandths

_____

6. four hundred twenty-two thousandths

_____

7. three and six hundred twelve thousandths

_____

Write in written form.

8. 0.009

_____

9. 0.067

_____

10. 0.723

_____

11. 3.614

_____

Mixed Applications

12. Jeremy lifts a 12-lb barbell 8 times per set. He does 3 sets. How many total pounds does Jeremy lift?

_____

13. Izeta's time for the 100-meter dash was 11.824 seconds. In what place-value position is the digit 4?

_____

Place Value

Write in standard form.

1. 5,000 + 400 + 30 + 7 + 0.6 + 0.01 + 0.009

_____

2. six thousand, seven hundred six and four hundred thirty-five thousandths

_____

3. 7,000 + 300 + 0 + 0 + 0.1 + 0.07 + 0.002

_____

4. two thousand, seventy seven and eight hundred six thousandths

_____

Write the value of the digit 6 in each number.

5. 3,628.314

_____

6. 4,921.567

_____

7. 7,847.126

_____

8. 9,761.478

_____

Mixed Applications

For Problems 9–11, use the table.

9. Write Albaro's time in written form.

_____

_____

10. Write Armstrong's time in expanded form.

_____

_____

1-MILE RUN	
Runner	**Time in seconds**
Harris	237.050
Armstrong	237.255
Albaro	240.005

11. Who won the 1-mile run? Who placed second?

_____

_____

Equivalent Decimals

Vocabulary

Fill in the blank.

1. _____ _____ are different names for the same number or amount.

Write *equivalent* or *not equivalent* to describe each set of decimals.

2. 0.4   and   .40

_____

3. 0.08   and   0.008

_____

Write an equivalent decimal for each.

4. 1.2 _____

5. 3.71 _____

6. 0.060 _____

7. 6.200 _____

8. 3.450 _____

9. 4.15 _____

10. 2.4 _____

11. 7.30 _____

12. 2.900 _____

Mixed Applications

13. Vinny won the 400-meter race in 48.69 seconds. Write an equivalent decimal for his time.

_____

14. Jami's family drove 175.6 miles to a vacation spot. Write an equivalent decimal for the distance they traveled.

_____

15. Dennis had 9 rebounds in each of his team's 15 games. What was the total number of rebounds for Dennis?

_____

16. What number has 8 in the thousand and thousandths place, 7 in the hundreds and hundredths place, 4 in the tens and tenths place, and 0 in the ones place?

_____

Comparing and Ordering

Use the number line to compare the decimals.

3.0   3.1   3.2   3.3   3.4   3.5   3.6   3.7   3.8   3.9   4.0

1. 3.62 ◯ 3.26   **2.** 3.20 ◯ 3.02   **3.** 3.59 ◯ 3.6

4. 3.30 ◯ 3.4   **5.** 3.54 ◯ 3.45   **6.** 3.15 ◯ 3.25

Write <, >, or = in each ◯.

7. 0.25 ◯ 0.23   **8.** 6.56 ◯ 6.65   **9.** 7.21 ◯ 7.210

10. 27.35 ◯ 27.53   **11.** 368.58 ◯ 368.85   **12.** 237.524 ◯ 237.254

13. 736.54 ◯ 736.540   **14.** 16.2 ◯ 16.200   **15.** 878.787 ◯ 878.878

Order from least to greatest.

16. 7.11, 7.09, 7.07   **17.** 12.54, 12.45, 12.65   **18.** 3.020, 3.002, 3.200

_____   _____   _____

19. 17.560, 17.065, 17.056   **20.** 2.654, 2.546, 2.456, 2.465

_____   _____

Mixed Applications

For Problems 21–23, use the menu.

21. Which sandwiches cost more than turkey but less than chicken?

_____

22. What is the cost of a ham and a tuna sandwich?

_____

23. Write the sandwiches in order from the least expensive to the most expensive.

_____

_____

Sandwich Menu	
Turkey	$2.65
Tuna	$2.95
Chicken	$3.25
Ham	$2.75
Cheese	$2.25

24. The swim team had $500 to spend on equipment. After spending $367, how much does the team have left to spend?

_____

Problem-Solving Strategy

Make a Table

Make a table and solve.

1. Three friends compared their batting averages. Jane batted 0.321, Nick batted 0.231, and Fred batted 0.312. Who had the highest average?

2. On a hot summer day in Arizona, the temperature was 115.6°F in Scottsdale, 116.5°F in Phoenix, and 115.9°F in Sun City. Where was the highest temperature?

3. The local deli offers three sandwiches. Tuna costs $3.25, turkey costs $2.95, and ham costs $3.35. Which sandwich is the most expensive?

4. Three students were in the high-jump competition. Mark jumped 1.54 meters, Peter jumped 1.45 meters, and Nader jumped 1.61 meters. Who made the highest jump?

Mixed Applications

Solve.

CHOOSE A STRATEGY

• Use a Table   • Work Backward   • Draw a Diagram   • Write a Number Sentence   • Guess and Check

5. Fredrica's car gets 24 miles to a gallon of gasoline. Its tank holds 19 gallons of gasoline. How far can the car be driven on one tank of gas?

6. Five students stand in a line. Ned is in the middle. Bart stands next to Ned. Lisa is at the right end. Matt stands between Ned and Lisa. Where is Margie?

7. Terri scored twice as many points in the second half of a basketball game than in the first half. She scored 24 second-half points. How many total points did Terri score?

8. Last year in Detroit it snowed 21.8 cm in December, 17.4 cm in January, 41.3 cm in February, and 24.9 cm in March. In which month did the most snow fall?

Adding Decimals

Use base-ten blocks to model. Record the sum on a place-value chart.

1.   0.2
    + 0.9

2.   0.23
    + 0.35

3.   1.251
    + 0.833

Find the sum.

4.   9.2
  +0.8

5.   7.2
  +3.6

6.   8.94
  +2.06

7.   1.257
  +3.333

8.   1.125
  +5.725

9.   2.4
  +1.5

10.   3.2
  +5.6

11.   1.38
  +0.91

12.   1.523
  +0.374

13.   3.682
  +2.479

14. $3.2 + 1.4 =$ _____

15. $2.68 + 3.14 =$ _____

16. $4.098 + 1.875 =$ _____

17. $5.7 + 3.6 =$ _____

18. $8.05 + 3.52 =$ _____

19. $1.111 + 2.222 =$ _____

Mixed Applications

20. Greg went to the store. He bought a bag of raisins for $1.29 and a carton of juice for $0.85. How much did he spend?

21. Susan found $0.63 in change. Her brother found $0.57. Together how much money did they find?

22. The art teacher Mr. Terry bought 25 blue pencils, 35 red pencils, and 48 green pencils. How many pencils did he buy in all?

23. Brad's family traveled 250 miles on Monday and 345 miles on Tuesday. Grace's family traveled 187 miles on Monday and 432 miles on Tuesday. Which family traveled more miles?

More About Adding Decimals

Use an equivalent decimal to find the sum.

1. 1.24 + 0.317 = _____

2. 2.082 + 3.6 = _____

3. 1.38 + 3.849 = _____

4. 2.54 + 3 = _____

5. 35.7 + 12.426 = _____

6. 37.84 + 6.592 = _____

7. 3.12 + 6 = _____

8. 21.3 + 15.264 = _____

9. 29.04 + 9.846 = _____

10.   7
   + 0.3

11.   4.6
   + 1.54

12.   4.06
   + 0.873

13.   8
   + 4.75

14.   6.344
   + 0.22

15.   5
   + 0.6

16.   3.9
   + 2.61

17.   7.04
   + 0.984

18.   6
   + 5.267

19.   2.841
   + 0.13

20.   2.5
   + 3.47

21.   3.1
   + 2.73

22.   8.4
   + 5.283

23.   7.683
   + 2.3

24.   13.2
   + 4.08

25.   7.03
   + 4.2

26.   8.35
   + 0.294

27.   9.2
   + 8.416

28.   4.257
   + 5.5

29.   21.3
   + 6.42

Mixed Applications

30. Tony rides his bike in the mountains. He writes how far he rides each day in his weekly log. How many miles did he ride this week?

Weekly Biking Log				
Mon	Tue	Wed	Thur	Fri
2.5 mi	1.6 mi	3.7 mi	1.8 mi	2.1 mi

_____

31. Samantha bought a new pair of ski gloves for $4.95 and 2 scarves for $2.78 each. How much did she spend for all her purchases?

_____

32. Roger sold 258 tickets to the school play. Fredrica sold 392 tickets. How many more tickets did Fredrica sell than Roger?

_____

Subtracting Decimals

Find the difference.

1.	2.5 $- 0.8$	2.	3.4 $- 3.1$	3.	2.04 $- 1.7$	4.	3.6 $- 2.7$	5.	3.5 $- 1.04$

6.	1.6 $- 0.8$	7.	4.8 $- 4.2$	8.	3.07 $- 2.8$	9.	4.2 $- 3.8$	10.	6.7 $- 2.02$

11.	3.87 $- 1.36$	12.	2.7 $- 1.824$	13.	5.426 $- 2.56$	14.	12.537 $- 4.315$	15.	19.469 $- 12.253$

16.	4.68 $- 2.15$	17.	3.2 $- 2.451$	18.	7.264 $- 3.49$	19.	16.852 $- 8.231$	20.	17.578 $- 13.154$

21. $2.36 - 1.17 =$ _____ **22.** $1.7 - 0.763 =$ _____ **23.** $2.8 - 1.9 =$ _____

24. $3.75 - 2.68 =$ _____ **25.** $2.4 - 1.468 =$ _____ **26.** $3.1 - 2.5 =$ _____

27. $3.68 - 1.892 =$ _____ **28.** $5.2 - 3.181 =$ _____ **29.** $6.42 - 3.374 =$ _____

30. $4.21 - 2.362 =$ _____ **31.** $7.3 - 4.226 =$ _____ **32.** $5.69 - 2.473 =$ _____

Mixed Applications

For Problems 33–35, use the table.

33. The maximum speeds of animals over one-quarter mile varies greatly. What is the difference between the fastest and the slowest animal?

_____

Speeds of Animals	
Quarter horse	47.5 mph
Greyhound	39.35 mph
Human	27.89 mph
Snail	0.03 mph

34. How much faster is a greyhound than a human?

_____

35. In the snail's speed, what is the place value of the 3?

_____

Estimating Sums and Differences

Estimate the sum or difference to the nearest tenth.

1.	6.45	2.	7.32	3.	7.68	4.	18.07	5.	27.36
	− 2.81		− 5.14		+ 3.52		+ 11.66		− 15.04

Estimate the sum or difference to the nearest hundredth.

6.	1.285	7.	2.843	8.	4.060	9.	6.341	10.	2.578
	+ 0.822		+ 7.158		− 3.724		− 1.636		− 0.372

Estimate the sum or difference and compare. Write $<$ or $>$ in each $\bigcirc$.

11. $7.21 - 5.56 \bigcirc 6.89 - 2.34$ **12.** $4.73 + 3.29 \bigcirc 5.32 + 2.99$

13. $9.213 + 4.764 \bigcirc 8.345 + 6.754$ **14.** $36.84 - 15.49 \bigcirc 58.94 - 37.99$

15. $45.76 + 21.84 \bigcirc 32.98 + 34.05$ **16.** $52.85 + 34.76 \bigcirc 46.34 + 39.82$

17. $9.034 - 4.571 \bigcirc 7.562 - 2.199$ **18.** $6.045 - 2.374 \bigcirc 8.461 - 5.921$

Mixed Applications

For Problems 19–21, use the table.

19. Value-Mart and Save-More both advertise that they have the lowest prices in town. Which store offers the best price on pretzels? How much less is the cost per ounce?

_____

COMPARISON SHOPPING		
	Value-Mart	**Save-More**
Pretzels	0.326¢ per ounce	0.33¢ per ounce
Cheese	$1.095 per pound	$1.113 per pound

20. Maria and Sara compared the price of cheese. In which store is the cheese more expensive? How much more expensive per pound is it?

_____

21. Sara spent $3.14 on pretzels and $5.89 on cheese. About how much did Sara spend in all?

_____

Name _____

Choosing Addition or Subtraction

Choose and name the operation. Solve.

1. Grace and Shelly are practicing for the marathon. Grace runs 23.8 miles and Shelly runs 19.9 miles. How many more miles does Grace run than Shelly?

_____

2. Jim buys two slot cars and tests them on a local track. The blue car has a lap time of 6.987 seconds and the red car has a lap time of 8.732 seconds. Which car is faster? How much faster?

_____

3. Jim is visiting his grandparents. It is 85.7 miles from his house to their house. If he drives there and back, how many miles does he travel?

_____

4. Tony buys a collector's set of baseball cards for $32.75. His mother buys him a set for $45.98. How much money do he and his mother spend on baseball cards?

_____

For Problems 5–7, use the items shown below.

5. Sue went shopping at the annual clearance sale. She bought a shirt and 2 pairs of socks. How much money did Sue spend?

_____

$4.58 $5.89 $9.76 $0.89 $9.50 $11.34

6. Sue paid for her clothes with a $20 bill. How much change did she receive?

_____

7. Tom bought a hat. His change was $5.24. How much money did he have to start with?

_____

Mixed Applications

8. Sal and Alice planted trees for the Forestry Service. Last weekend Sal planted 113 trees and Alice planted 97 trees. How many more trees did Sal plant?

_____

9. Cheryl wants to put a border around her window. The window is $3\frac{1}{2}$ feet wide and $5\frac{1}{4}$ feet high. How much border does she need to go around the window?

_____

Problem-Solving Strategy

Write a Number Sentence

Write number sentences to solve.

1. Devin's checking account has a starting balance of $78.15. He writes checks for $15.78, $23.89, and $5.10. He makes 1 deposit of $68.00. What is his balance? Does he have enough to write a check for $90.00?

2. Lisa's bank statement shows a balance of $23.75. The statement shows deposits of $67.35 and $150.00. She writes checks for $55.00 and $62.88. What is Lisa's current balance?

_____

3. Ingrid can run a 100-meter dash in 10.49 seconds. Will her team beat the 400-meter record of 41.37 seconds if her 3 teammates also run 100 meters in 10.49 seconds?

4. At the paper airplane derby, the team from Flight Town U.S.A. has hang times of 11.7 seconds, 9.6 seconds, 10.5 seconds, and 12.3 seconds. What is the team's total hang time?

_____

Mixed Applications

Solve.

CHOOSE A STRATEGY

• Use a Table • Draw a Diagram • Guess and Check • Work Backward • Write a Number Sentence

For Problems 5–6, use the table.

5. Tina traveled with her father in his truck. His truck travels about 450 miles on 1 tank of gas. About how many tanks of gas did they use in the fourth week?

Weekly Miles Driven	
Week 1	1,832
Week 2	2,164
Week 3	1,624
Week 4	857

6. Tina spends all but the third week traveling with her father. How many miles does Tina ride with her father during the month?

7. Did Tina and her father drive more in weeks 1 and 2 or in weeks 3 and 4? How much more?

_____

Using Multiplication Properties

Vocabulary

Write the correct letter from Column 2.

Column 1

___ **1.** Zero Property for Multiplication

___ **2.** Property of One

___ **3.** Associative Property of Multiplication

___ **4.** Commutative Property of Multiplication

Column 2

a. When one of the factors is 1, the product equals the other number.

b. You can group factors differently. The product is always the same.

c. When one factor is 0, the product is 0.

d. You can multiply numbers in any order. The product is always the same.

Write the name of the multiplication property used in each number sentence.

5. $2 \times 6 = 6 \times 2$ 　　**6.** $(4 \times 2) \times 5 = 4 \times (2 \times 5)$ 　　**7.** $7 \times 1 = 7$

_____　　_____　　_____

Complete the equation. Identify the property used.

8. $3 \times \boxed{} = 0$ 　　**9.** $\boxed{} \times 7 = 7 \times 6$ 　　**10.** $(5 \times 4) \times 3 = 5 \times (\boxed{} \times 3)$

_____　　_____　　_____

Mixed Applications

11. It takes Mel 23 minutes to walk to school. It takes Julia 17 minutes to walk to school. How much longer does it take Mel to get to school than Julia?

12. In Mr. Pod's class, there are 6 desks with 3 students at each desk. In Ms. Carter's class, there are 7 desks with 2 students at each desk. Which classroom has more students?

_____　　_____

Recording Multiplication

Explain how you would model with colored counters.

1. $\begin{array}{r} 304 \\ \times\ 4 \\ \hline \end{array}$	2. $\begin{array}{r} 461 \\ \times\ 5 \\ \hline \end{array}$	3. $\begin{array}{r} 200 \\ \times\ 6 \\ \hline \end{array}$	4. $\begin{array}{r} 705 \\ \times\ 2 \\ \hline \end{array}$

_____ _____ _____ _____

_____ _____ _____ _____

_____ _____ _____ _____

_____ _____ _____ _____

Solve by using colored counters.

5. $2 \times 156 = n$ 6. $3 \times 450 = n$ 7. $4 \times 392 = n$ 8. $6 \times 378 = n$

_____   _____   _____   _____

Mixed Applications

For Problem 11, use the table.

9. Frank and Felicia arrived at the restaurant at 7:00 P.M. They stayed for 1 hour. It took them 10 minutes to get home, 15 minutes to pay the baby-sitter, and 30 minutes to get the kids to bed. What time were the kids in bed?

_____

10. Sam rode his bike to school each day for 29 days. The total distance each day was 5 miles. Ariel rode her bike to school each day for 20 days. The total distance each day was 8 miles. Who rode a greater distance?

_____

11. Tamara and David went out to lunch on Thursday. They each bought a slice of pizza, a salad, and a drink. How much did they spend in all?

_____

Lunch Prices	
Pizza	$1.25
Salad	$1.75
Drink	$1.10
Chips	$0.70

Name _____

Practicing Multiplication

Find the product.

1. $\begin{array}{r} 315 \\ \times\ \ 3 \\ \hline \end{array}$	**2.** $\begin{array}{r} 421 \\ \times\ \ 8 \\ \hline \end{array}$	**3.** $\begin{array}{r} 526 \\ \times\ \ 9 \\ \hline \end{array}$	**4.** $\begin{array}{r} 137 \\ \times\ \ 2 \\ \hline \end{array}$
5. $\begin{array}{r} 213 \\ \times\ \ 6 \\ \hline \end{array}$	**6.** $\begin{array}{r} 336 \\ \times\ \ 4 \\ \hline \end{array}$	**7.** $\begin{array}{r} 554 \\ \times\ \ 7 \\ \hline \end{array}$	**8.** $\begin{array}{r} 692 \\ \times\ \ 5 \\ \hline \end{array}$

9. $428 \times 8 = n$

10. $361 \times 3 = n$

11. $603 \times 5 = n$

12. $830 \times 9 = n$

13. $531 \times 6 = n$

14. $222 \times 4 = n$

15. $651 \times 6 = n$

16. $108 \times 9 = n$

17. $752 \times 4 = n$

18. $903 \times 6 = n$

19. $362 \times 4 = n$

20. $841 \times 2 = n$

Mixed Applications

21. Janet and Alan have 236 stamps. They collect 20 more each day for 3 days. What is the total amount of stamps they have at the end of 3 days?

22. Tomika had $15.23. She went to the store and bought an eraser, notebook, stapler, and pencils for $12.35. How much change did she get back?

23. Suzie plays basketball. Her team's total for the season is 409 points. They scored the following points in their first 4 games: 80, 85, 76, and 83. How many points did they score in their fifth game?

24. Jacob does 125 sit-ups each day. He does them for a week. How many sit-ups does he do in one week?

Finding Volume

Vocabulary

Fill in the blanks.

1. The measure of the space a solid figure occupies is _____.

2. Volume is measured in _____.

Tell how many unit cubes were used to build each rectangular prism.
Find the volume.

3.

units

_____

volume

_____

4.

units

_____

volume

_____

5.

units

_____

volume

_____

6.

units

_____

volume

_____

Use unit cubes to build each prism. Complete the table.

	Length of Base	Height Width of Base	(number of layers)	Volume (cubic units)
7.	7 cubes	3 cubes	5 cubes	_____
8.	6 cubes	2 cubes	4 cubes	_____
9.	8 cubes	4 cubes	3 cubes	_____

Mixed Applications

10. Shana has two shoe boxes. One shoe box is $4 \times 3 \times 5$ cubic units. The other shoe box is $3 \times 4 \times 6$ cubic units. Which shoe box has the larger volume?

_____

11. Tim receives $1.25 for every piece of trash he picks up. He picks up 9 pieces on Monday and 8 pieces on Tuesday. How much money does Tim earn?

_____

Finding Area and Volume

Vocabulary

Fill in the blank.

1. A _____ is a set of symbols that expresses a mathematical rule.

   The formula for area is Area = length × width, or $A = l \times w$.

   The formula for volume is Volume = length × width × height, or $V = l \times w \times h$.

Find the area.

2.
   6 in.
   10 in.

_____

3. l = 36 cm

   w = 4 cm

   $A = \boxed{}$ sq cm

_____

4. l = 16 m

   w = 3 m

   $A = \boxed{}$ sq m

_____

Find the volume.

5.
   9 in.
   6 in.
   3 in.

_____

6. l = 5 cm

   w = 7 cm

   h = 8 cm

   $v = \boxed{}$ cu cm

_____

7. l = 4 in.

   w = 6 in.

   h = 8 in.

   $v = \boxed{}$ cu in.

_____

Mixed Applications

8. There are 22 students in Mr. Petri's fourth grade class. Each student has 4 textbooks. How many textbooks are there in all?

_____

_____

9. Tom's shelf is 6 feet long, 4 feet wide, and 3 feet high. Kim's shelf is 7 feet long, 4 feet wide, and 4 feet high. Who has the shelf with the larger volume? Explain.

_____

_____

Use a Formula

Use a formula to solve.

1. Keesha is painting a mural. The wall is 11 feet long and 8 feet wide. What is the area of the wall that Keesha is painting?

_____

2. The Carreys are fencing in their backyard. The fence measures 18 feet long and 9 feet wide. What is the area of their backyard?

_____

3. Chelsey sees two doghouses to buy. One measures 4 ft × 4 ft × 3 ft. The other measures 3 ft × 5 ft × 5 ft. She wants to get the one with the larger volume. Which doghouse should she buy?

_____

4. Ron likes two dressers with the same features. One measures 4 ft × 4 ft × 2 ft and costs $76. The other measures 3 ft × 5 ft × 2 ft and costs $85. Which dresser is the better buy?

_____

Mixed Applications

Solve.

CHOOSE A STRATEGY

- **Draw a Diagram**
- **Write a Number Sentence**
- **Use a Table**
- **Make a Model**

5. Kim walks 3 miles to the playground and 3 miles home. She walks there and back 4 days a week. How many miles does she walk in a week?

_____

6. Hank's vegetable garden measures 8 feet long and 6 feet wide. He starts at one corner and plants marigolds along the edge. The marigolds are 1 foot apart. How many marigolds does he plant?

_____

7. Jeanette has $52.00. She wants to buy a coat for $35.69, a scarf for $8.99, and a pair of gloves for $5.50. What is the total cost for all those items? Does she have enough money?

_____

_____

8. Lauren wants to buy an aquarium that has a volume of 18 cubic units. How many different aquariums with the same volume could she buy? Write the measurements for each one.

_____

_____

Using the Distributive Property

Vocabulary

Fill in the blanks.

1. The _____ _____ allows
   you to break apart numbers to make them easy to multiply.

Use the grid below to model. Find the product.

2. $10 \times 17 = n$

3. $15 \times 14 = n$

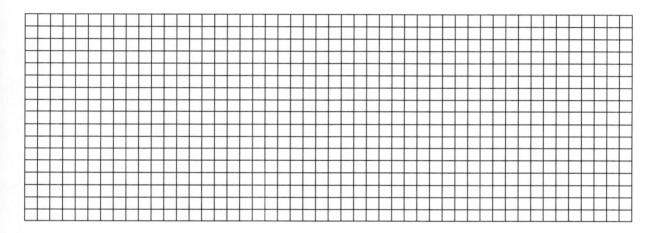

Use the Distributive Property to rewrite each equation. Find the product.

4. $12 \times 18 = n$

5. $20 \times 23 = n$

6. $30 \times 33 = n$

_____ $n =$

_____ $n =$

_____ $n =$

_____

_____

_____

_____

_____

_____

_____

_____

_____

Mixed Applications

7. A tennis player serves the ball at a speed of 95.42 miles per hour. What does the 2 digit stand for?

8. Every week, Jan runs 19 miles on Monday through Thursday and 17 miles on Saturday. How many miles does she run in a week?

_____

_____

Multiplying by Two-Digit Numbers

Find the product.

1.   16
  $\times$ 12

2.   17
  $\times$ 15

3.   18
  $\times$ 14

4.   20
  $\times$ 18

5.   24
  $\times$ 16

6.   45
  $\times$ 25

7.   80
  $\times$ 35

8.   125
  $\times$ 30

9.   24
  $\times$ 46

10.   16
  $\times$ 37

11.   43
  $\times$ 54

12.   74
  $\times$ 47

Mixed Applications

13. A bus company has 36 buses. Each bus can hold 54 people. How many people can the bus company serve in all?

_____

14. Ralph's car gets 24 miles to a gallon of gas. Its tank holds 16 gallons of gas. How far can Ralph's car go on one tank of gas?

_____

15. Seth, Brian, and Mark are comparing their heights. At 52 inches, Seth is 6 inches taller than Brian. Brian is 3 inches shorter than Mark. How tall is Mark?

_____

16. Racers can choose from 4 brands of sports drinks. Each brand comes in 5 flavors. What is the total number of drink choices?

_____

Estimating Products

Estimate the product by rounding each factor to its greatest place-value position.

1. 104
    × 35   × _____

2. 125
    × 49   × _____

3. 162
    × 66   × _____

4. 175
    × 75   × _____

5. 215
    × 51   × _____

6. 348
    × 81   × _____

7. 455
    × 55   × _____

8. 496
    × 64   × _____

9. 549
    × 49   × _____

10. $38 \times 562 = n$

11. $35 \times 735 = n$

12. $86 \times 860 = n$

_____   _____   _____

13. $56 \times 479 = n$

14. $28 \times 358 = n$

15. $42 \times 734 = n$

_____   _____   _____

Mixed Applications

16. At the garden center, there were 174 rows of flowers. Each row contained 86 flowers. Estimate the number of flowers in all.

17. Joel's dad sold his paintings for $750 each. He sold 26 paintings at a show. Estimate how much money in all Joel's dad made.

18. The Palmers have a large freezer that measures 6 feet long by 2 feet wide and 2 feet tall. What is the volume of the freezer?

19. Sharon spent $2 on a magazine; then she spent half of the rest of her money on shoes. She spent half of her remaining money on lunch. She has $12 left. How much did Sharon start with?

Multiplying by Three-Digit Numbers

Estimate to the greatest place-value position. Then find the product.

1.
$$\begin{array}{r} 126 \\ \times \quad 115 \end{array}$$ × _____

2.
$$\begin{array}{r} 174 \\ \times \quad 149 \end{array}$$ × _____

3.
$$\begin{array}{r} 243 \\ \times \quad 176 \end{array}$$ × _____

4.
$$\begin{array}{r} 339 \\ \times \quad 264 \end{array}$$ × _____

5.
$$\begin{array}{r} 456 \\ \times \quad 349 \end{array}$$ × _____

6.
$$\begin{array}{r} 627 \\ \times \quad 495 \end{array}$$ × _____

7.
$$\begin{array}{r} 1,495 \\ \times \quad 627 \end{array}$$ × _____

8.
$$\begin{array}{r} 2,501 \\ \times \quad 251 \end{array}$$ × _____

9.
$$\begin{array}{r} 2,328 \\ \times \quad 346 \end{array}$$ × _____

10. $408 \times 562 = n$

11. $329 \times 1,123 = n$

12. $2,147 \times 415 = n$

_____

_____

_____

13. $336 \times 483 = n$

14. $212 \times 3,678 = n$

15. $4,552 \times 53 = n$

_____

_____

_____

Mixed Applications

16. Terri consumes an average of 2,200 calories a day. About how many calories in all will she consume in a year?

17. Brian earns $440 a week. If he works 48 weeks a year, how much will he earn this year?

_____

_____

Multiplying to Find Perimeter and Area

Multiply to find the perimeter and area for each figure.

1.
125 cm

85 cm

_____

_____

2.
136 m

174 m

_____

_____

3.
345 in.

176 in.

_____

_____

4.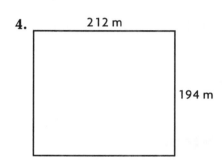
212 m

194 m

_____

_____

5.
92 ft

388 ft

_____

_____

6.
142 yd

326 yd

_____

_____

7. The school banner is 140 inches by 68 inches. What are its perimeter and area?

_____

8. If 325 people run a 13-mile race, how many miles in all are run by the runners?

_____

Problem-Solving Strategy

Draw a Diagram

Draw a diagram to solve.

1. Cedric has 52 feet of wood to use to make a rectangular garden. He wants the garden to have the greatest possible area. What dimensions should it have?

2. Darci has 68 feet of fencing to use to make a pen for her dog. She wants her dog to have the greatest possible play area. What dimensions should the pen have?

3. Tamara walks 4 blocks north, 2 blocks east, and 4 blocks south. How would she walk back to where she started?

4. Anoki is building a fence to enclose an 18 × 24 meter rectangular area. The fence needs a post every 6 meters. How many posts does Anoki need?

Mixed Applications

Solve.

| CHOOSE A STRATEGY |

• Draw a Diagram • Write a Number Sentence • Use a Formula • Make a Table • Guess and Check

5. Mrs. Saturno's classroom is 23 feet × 18 feet. Mr. Downing's classroom is 22 feet × 19 feet. Whose classroom has the greater area?

6. It takes Ben 8 minutes to read one chapter of a book. How long will it take him to read 12 chapters?

7. Mt. Marcy has an elevation of 5,344 ft. The elevation of Mt. Washington is 6,288 ft; Mt. Olympus, 7,965 ft; and Mt. Katahdin, 5,268 ft. Which mountain has the highest elevation? the lowest?

8. Wilma has two containers. One is 10 in. × 4 in. × 8 in. The other is 9 in. × 6 in. × 6 in. Together, will they hold 700 cubic inches of jelly beans?

Divisibility

Vocabulary

Fill in the blank.

1. A number is _____ by another number if
   the quotient is a whole number and there is a zero remainder.

Use mental math and a calculator. Test each number for
divisibility by 2, 3, 4, 5, 6, 9, and 10. List the numbers that work.

2. 54

3. 144

4. 420

5. 864

_____

6. 990

7. 1,224

8. 3,600

9. 6,618

_____

10. 234

11. 684

12. 1,827

13. 2,475

_____

14. 675

15. 288

16. 842

17. 540

_____

Mixed Applications

18. Marie made 3 dozen cookies.
    She needs to divide them evenly
    into groups greater than 4. What
    are all the possible equal-size
    groups into which she can divide
    the cookies?

19. Ted needs to divide 60 stickers
    into equal groups. What are all the
    possible equal-size groups into
    which he can divide the stickers?

20. A box is 7 feet long, 4 feet wide,
    and 3 feet high. What is the
    volume of the box?

21. I am a number between 55 and
    65. I am divisible by 2, 3, 4, 5, 6,
    10, and 12. What number am I?

Placing the First Digit

Vocabulary

Fill in the blanks.

1. _____ are numbers
close to the actual numbers that can be divided evenly.

_____

Estimate the quotient.

2. $817 \div 4 \approx n$ 3. $462 \div 9 \approx n$ 4. $703 \div 7 \approx n$ 5. $492 \div 8 \approx n$

_____   _____   _____   _____

6. $281 \div 3 \approx n$ 7. $539 \div 6 \approx n$ 8. $925 \div 3 \approx n$ 9. $293 \div 5 \approx n$

_____   _____   _____   _____

Find the quotient.

10. $3\overline{)144}$ 11. $6\overline{)174}$ 12. $9\overline{)153}$ 13. $7\overline{)476}$

14. $2\overline{)249}$ 15. $4\overline{)855}$ 16. $7\overline{)799}$ 17. $8\overline{)975}$

Mixed Applications

18. Seth saved $234 during the past
6 months. Each month, he saved
the same amount. How much did
Seth save each month?

19. Rita made 150 ounces of soup.
She poured the soup into 8-ounce
containers. How many containers
did she fill? How many ounces of
soup were left over?

_____   _____

Zeros in Division

Estimate the quotient.

1. $8\overline{)330}$
2. $6\overline{)371}$
3. $2\overline{)813}$
4. $9\overline{)625}$

Find the quotient.

5. $5\overline{)535}$
6. $3\overline{)924}$
7. $4\overline{)836}$
8. $6\overline{)615}$

9. $2\overline{)610}$
10. $9\overline{)960}$
11. $7\overline{)423}$
12. $8\overline{)647}$

13. $902 \div 9 = n$
14. $409 \div 2 = n$
15. $142 \div 5 = n$
16. $821 \div 8 = n$

_____ _____ _____ _____

Mixed Applications

17. On Saturday and Sunday, a total of 908 people attended the museum. If the same number of people came each day, how many went to the museum on Sunday?

_____

18. During a 5-hour period, 510 lunches were sold in a cafeteria. If the same number of lunches were sold each hour, how many lunches were sold during the first hour?

_____

19. There are 24 teams in a soccer league. If there are 15 players on each team, how many players are in the league?

_____

20. I am a number between 30 and 40. I am divisible by 2, 3, 4, 6, and 9. What number am I?

_____

Practicing Division

Use divisibility rules to predict if there will be a remainder.

1. $4\overline{)832}$ 2. $2\overline{)417}$ 3. $7\overline{)217}$ 4. $6\overline{)213}$

_____   _____   _____   _____

Find the quotient. Check by multiplying.

5. $9\overline{)326}$ 6. $3\overline{)235}$ 7. $6\overline{)367}$ 8. $4\overline{)935}$

9. $6\overline{)115}$ 10. $9\overline{)504}$ 11. $7\overline{)219}$ 12. $5\overline{)621}$

13. $517 \div 2 = n$ 14. $609 \div 3 = n$ 15. $785 \div 7 = n$ 16. $431 \div 6 = n$

_____   _____   _____   _____

Mixed Applications

17. On Friday and Saturday, 618 people attended a car show. If the same number of people went each day, how many people attended the car show on Saturday?

_____

18. Abby rode her bike 15.73 miles. Carla rode twice as far as Abby. How many miles did Carla ride? How many miles did they ride in all?

_____

19. Sue drove 364 miles in 7 hours. How many miles did she drive in 1 hour?

_____

20. John paid for lunch with a $20.00 bill. He received $14.37 in change. How much money did he spend for lunch?

_____

Interpreting the Remainder

Solve. Explain how you interpreted the remainder.

1. A total of 134 players signed up for a soccer league. The league has 9 teams. How many players will be on most of the teams?

_____

_____

2. There are 230 books in the storeroom. The books are stored in 7 boxes. How many books are in most of the boxes?

_____

_____

3. Lauren's piece of wire is 5 times longer than Larry's wire. Lauren's wire is 8 cm long. How long is Larry's wire?

_____

_____

4. Lee's Bakery sells muffins by the dozen. The bakery has 230 muffins prepared. Does the bakery have enough muffins to fill 20 orders?

_____

_____

5. Sue has 85 flowers. She put them in 7 vases with the same number of flowers in each vase except one. How many flowers are in the vase with the greatest number of flowers?

_____

_____

6. Jeremy had 75 feet of string. He divided it into 4 equal pieces. How long was each piece of string?

_____

_____

Mixed Applications

7. Each player on the soccer team has 32 raffle tickets to sell. There are 15 players on the team. How many tickets do they have to sell in all?

_____

_____

8. For a fund-raising project, 8 students need to sell 500 boxes of cookies. How many boxes does each student get to sell? How many boxes are left over?

_____

_____

Problem-Solving Strategy

Guess and Check

Guess and check to solve.

1. Scott is 5 years old. His Aunt Mary is 4 times as old. How old will Scott be when he is half as old as his aunt?

2. The sum of two numbers is 42. Their product is 360. What are the two numbers?

3. A tunnel toll is $1.25 for cars and $2.00 for trucks. In one hour, $40.00 is collected from 23 vehicles. How many cars and trucks paid the toll?

4. Bob has 276 baseball cards. He keeps them in equal groups in boxes, and has started a new box with 3 cards in it. How many boxes of cards does he have? How many baseball cards are in each box?

Mixed Applications

Solve.

┌─ **CHOOSE A STRATEGY** ─┐

• **Use a Formula** • **Write a Number Sentence** • **Make a Table** • **Guess and Check**

5. There were 123 cupcakes, brownies, and muffins for sale at the bake sale. There were twice as many brownies as muffins. There were 37 muffins. How many cupcakes were for sale?

6. Kelly rides her horse 1 hour a day 3 times a week. She rides 40 minutes a day 2 times a week. On Saturdays she rides 1 hour 15 minutes. She doesn't ride on Sundays. How much time does Kelly spend riding her horse each week?

7. The Scouts washed 12 cars one afternoon. They earned $6.50 for each car they washed. How much money did they earn?

8. The fence around Jan's backyard is 45 feet long and 30 feet wide. What is the perimeter of the fence? What is the area of the yard?

Division Patterns to Estimate

Complete the pattern.

1. $100 \div 20 =$ _____

$1,000 \div 20 =$ _____

$10,000 \div 20 =$ _____

2. $900 \div 90 =$ _____

$9,000 \div 90 =$ _____

$90,000 \div 90 =$ _____

3. $300 \div 50 =$ _____

$3,000 \div 50 =$ _____

$30,000 \div 50 =$ _____

4. $140 \div 20 =$ _____

$1,400 \div 20 =$ _____

$14,000 \div 20 =$ _____

5. $250 \div 50 =$ _____

$2,500 \div 50 =$ _____

$25,000 \div 50 =$ _____

6. $360 \div 60 =$ _____

$3,600 \div 60 =$ _____

$36,000 \div 60 =$ _____

Find the quotient.

7. $120 \div 40 =$ _____

8. $240 \div 80 =$ _____

9. $810 \div 90 =$ _____

10. $350 \div 70 =$ _____

11. $480 \div 60 =$ _____

12. $720 \div 80 =$ _____

13. $4,000 \div 80 =$ _____

14. $2,000 \div 20 =$ _____

15. $4,500 \div 50 =$ _____

16. $21,000 \div 70 =$ _____

17. $63,000 \div 90 =$ _____

18. $54,000 \div 90 =$ _____

19. $36,000 \div 40 =$ _____

20. $12,000 \div 30 =$ _____

21. $24,000 \div 80 =$ _____

Mixed Applications

22. A classroom in Appleby School is 60 feet long. How long would a row of 30 classrooms be?

_____

23. There are 60 boxes of pencils in the school supply closet. Each box holds 50 pencils. How many pencils are there in all?

_____

24. In the month of April, Sam delivered a total of 1,200 newspapers during the 30 days. He delivered the same number of papers each day. How many papers did Sam deliver daily?

_____

25. Mark bought an ice-cream sundae for himself and one for each of his 3 friends. Each sundae cost $1.75. How much change did Mark get back from his $10 bill?

_____

Estimating Quotients

Write two pairs of compatible numbers for each. Give two
possible estimates.

1. $359 \div 55 = n$ **2.** $715 \div 74 = n$ **3.** $156 \div 37 = n$

_____   _____   _____

_____   _____   _____

4. $438 \div 57 = n$ **5.** $1{,}893 \div 52 = n$ **6.** $3{,}127 \div 44 = n$

_____   _____   _____

_____   _____   _____

Estimate the quotient.

7. $18\overline{)175}$ **8.** $37\overline{)231}$ **9.** $62\overline{)375}$ **10.** $81\overline{)255}$

11. $53\overline{)2{,}681}$ **12.** $41\overline{)3{,}289}$ **13.** $79\overline{)4{,}007}$ **14.** $29\overline{)1{,}811}$

15. $34\overline{)241}$ **16.** $53\overline{)4{,}787}$ **17.** $47\overline{)388}$ **18.** $68\overline{)3{,}594}$

Mixed Applications

19. There are 57 boxes of paper in
the school supply room. A total of
3,641 sheets of paper are in the
boxes. About how many sheets
of paper are in each box?

_____

20. Linda sold 19 boxes of cookies.
Dora sold twice as many boxes
as Linda sold. Eve sold 14 more
boxes than Dora did. How many
boxes did Eve sell?

_____

21. The Hawks soccer team scored
a total of 119 goals. The team
played 31 games. About how
many goals did the team score
each game?

_____

22. Seth has 423 baseball cards. His
brother Jon has 117 fewer cards.
How many cards does Jon have?

_____

Placing the First Digit

Estimate the quotient.

1. $7,311 \div 89 \approx n$ **2.** $5,602 \div 78 \approx n$ **3.** $2,109 \div 66 \approx n$

_____   _____   _____

4. $6,521 \div 77 \approx n$ **5.** $2,680 \div 26 \approx n$ **6.** $5,591 \div 92 \approx n$

_____   _____   _____

Draw a box where the first digit in the quotient should be placed.

7. $17\overline{)1,527}$ **8.** $23\overline{)1,941}$ **9.** $34\overline{)7,109}$ **10.** $45\overline{)5,683}$

11. $89\overline{)9,266}$ **12.** $31\overline{)6,683}$ **13.** $24\overline{)1,742}$ **14.** $87\overline{)9,556}$

Find the quotient.

15. $72\overline{)8,136}$ **16.** $39\overline{)4,579}$ **17.** $27\overline{)2,835}$ **18.** $49\overline{)7,116}$

19. $13\overline{)3,926}$ **20.** $81\overline{)9,446}$ **21.** $35\overline{)7,105}$ **22.** $26\overline{)3,109}$

Mixed Applications

23. A total of 560 people will be attending a dinner. The people will sit at tables of 16. How many tables should be set up?

_____

24. Alison rowed the canoe from 1:15 until 3:05. Then she rowed after dinner from 6:20 until 8:40. How long did she row in all?

_____

25. Larry has 612 baseball cards. He arranges his cards in albums that hold 36 cards each. How many albums has Larry filled?

_____

26. A bus can hold 48 passengers. A total of 14 buses are filled to take members of the garden club on a trip. How many people went on the trip?

_____

Correcting Quotients

Write *too high, too low,* or *just right* for each estimate.

1.
$$34\overline{)105}$$ quotient 2

_____

2.
$$17\overline{)89}$$ quotient 5

_____

3.
$$42\overline{)295}$$ quotient 8

_____

4.
$$23\overline{)119}$$ quotient 5

_____

5.
$$26\overline{)235}$$ quotient 9

_____

6.
$$36\overline{)291}$$ quotient 9

_____

7.
$$91\overline{)195}$$ quotient 3

_____

8.
$$56\overline{)327}$$ quotient 4

_____

Choose the better estimate to use in the quotient. Circle *a* or *b*.

9. $23\overline{)94}$ **a.** 4   **b.** 5

10. $41\overline{)173}$ **a.** 3   **b.** 4

11. $68\overline{)512}$ **a.** 7   **b.** 8

12. $58\overline{)311}$ **a.** 5   **b.** 6

Find the quotient.

13. $76\overline{)308}$

14. $23\overline{)711}$

15. $14\overline{)296}$

16. $39\overline{)177}$

17. $46\overline{)172}$

18. $29\overline{)544}$

19. $13\overline{)98}$

20. $57\overline{)382}$

Mixed Applications

21. A total of 635 people signed up for a bus trip. Each bus can hold 48 people. Will 13 buses be enough for the trip?

_____

22. The glee club sold 180 tickets for its annual luncheon. At the luncheon, people will sit at tables of 8. Will 22 tables be enough?

_____

23. A garden is 14 feet long and 11 feet wide. What is the area of the garden?

_____

24. The Smiths traveled 312 miles on Friday and 470 miles on Saturday. How many more miles did they travel on Saturday than on Friday?

_____

Name _____

Using Division

Divide. Check by multiplying.

1. $16\overline{)73}$
2. $37\overline{)85}$
3. $55\overline{)92}$
4. $79\overline{)317}$

5. $35\overline{)219}$
6. $96\overline{)742}$
7. $41\overline{)265}$
8. $27\overline{)116}$

9. $71\overline{)603}$
10. $54\overline{)449}$
11. $22\overline{)391}$
12. $67\overline{)465}$

13. $63\overline{)414}$
14. $37\overline{)218}$
15. $84\overline{)761}$
16. $52\overline{)786}$

17. $4{,}581 \div 32 = n$
18. $1{,}985 \div 23 = n$
19. $8{,}042 \div 91 = n$

_____   _____   _____

20. $5{,}401 \div 25 = n$
21. $1{,}933 \div 42 = n$
22. $3{,}751 \div 55 = n$

_____   _____   _____

Mixed Applications

23. The students at Walnut Street School collected 3,102 cans for a recycling center. Each student brought in 6 cans. How many students attend the school?

_____

24. The Sweet Shoppe sold 2,610 ice-cream cones during the 30 days of June. It sold the same number of cones each day. How many cones were sold per day?

_____

25. A box is 15 cm long, 9 cm wide, and 12 cm high. What is the volume of the box?

_____

26. There are 26 teams in a baseball league. Each team has 14 players. How many players are in the league?

_____

Choosing the Operation

Tell what operation should be used to solve each problem. Then solve.

1. Three school bands participated in a canned food drive. The Vikings collected 782 cans. The Spartans collected 1,298 cans. The Eagles collected 917 cans. How many cans did all three schools collect?

_____

2. A basketball league gives each team a dozen basketballs to use during the season. How many basketballs are needed if there are 26 teams in the league?

_____

3. Carlos arranges 34 blocks in a column. The total height of the column is 238 cm. How high is each block?

_____

4. Ricky earns $3,209 a month. Diana earns $4,022 a month. How much more money per month does Diana earn than Ricky?

_____

5. Seth needs two pieces of wire for a project. One piece must be 18 cm long, and the other piece must be 25 cm long. How much wire does Seth need for the project?

_____

6. Barbara has 418 stamps. Her sister Jean has 56 fewer stamps. How many stamps does Jean have?

_____

Mixed Applications

Solve.

7. At a movie theater, Gayle bought 5 adult tickets and 3 children's tickets. An adult ticket cost $5, and a child's ticket cost $3. How much money did Gayle spend?

_____

8. A clothing company manufactured 2,496 hats. The hats were distributed evenly among 52 stores. How many hats were sent to each store?

_____

Problem-Solving Strategy

Write a Number Sentence

Write a number sentence to solve.

1. Joel sells handmade birdhouses. He has 18 birdhouses for sale. The price of 10 birdhouses is $12 each, and 8 others sell for $10 each. If Joel sells all 18 birdhouses, how much money will he get?

_____

_____

2. Carole scored 9,024 on a computer game the first time she played it. Her score for the second game was 817 points less than her first score. What was Carole's score for the second game?

_____

_____

3. Dan bought a stereo for $972. He will pay it off in 18 months. What will his monthly payments be?

_____

_____

4. Rita has 645 stamps in her collection. She keeps them in albums. Each holds 48 stamps. How many albums does Rita have?

_____

_____

Mixed Applications

Solve.

CHOOSE A STRATEGY

• Use a Table • Act It Out • Guess and Check • Work Backward • Write a Number Sentence

5. Zach went to the mall and spent $6 on lunch, $8 on school supplies, and $5 playing video games. When he got home, Zach had $12 left. How much money did Zach start his day with?

_____

6. Oak School's gym holds 800 students. Can students in all three grades attend an assembly in the gym at the same time? Explain.

Student Enrollment	
Sixth grade	312
Seventh grade	237
Eighth grade	276

_____

Finding the Median and the Mode

Vocabulary

Write the correct letter from Column 2.

Column 1

Column 2

1. the middle number in an ordered series of numbers _____

a. median

2. the number that occurs the most often in a series of numbers _____

b. mode

Use index cards to find the median and the mode for each set of data. Write each set of numbers on the index cards.

3.

Julian's Test Scores							
Test	1	2	3	4	5	6	7
Score	86	98	98	85	87	92	89

4.

Students' Heights					
Name	Rose	Sally	Hank	John	Raj
Inches	57	53	55	56	57

5.

Baseball Cards					
Name	Sam	Jen	Tad	Phil	Li
Number	300	280	320	280	340

6.

Magazines Sold							
Week	1	2	3	4	5	6	7
Number	180	150	175	160	225	190	225

Mixed Applications

7. Sara practiced doing leg-lifts for 5 days. She did 25 leg-lifts the first day, 30 leg-lifts the next three days, and 55 leg-lifts the last day. What are the median and the mode for the number of leg-lifts Sara did?

8. There are 2 classes with 35 students in each. There are 3 classes with 32 students in each. What is the total number of students in the 5 classes?

Finding the Mean

Vocabulary

Complete.

1. The _____, or average, is a way to find one
   number that represents all the numbers in a set of data.

___

For Problems 2–3, use the stem-and-leaf plot.

2. Write the mean for Henry's test scores.

_____

3. Write the median and the mode.

_____

HENRY'S TEST SCORES	
Stem	**Leaves**
7	6 7 7
8	5 6 8
9	1 2 3

For Problems 4–5, use the table.

4. What is the mean for the number of students
   that attended the assembly each period?

_____

5. Write the median and the mode for the data.

_____

ASSEMBLY ATTENDANCE	
Period	**Number of Students**
First	220
Second	180
Third	160
Fourth	200
Fifth	160

Find the mean, median, and mode for each set of data.

6. 2, 8, 3, 8, 4   **7.** 30, 10, 20, 10, 10   **8.** 115, 110, 120, 100, 100

_____   _____   _____

_____   _____   _____

Mixed Applications

9. There are 5 children in the
   Hamilton family. Their ages are
   16, 14, 12, 9, 9. What are the mean,
   median, and mode for their ages?

10. There are 256 students going
    on a field trip. Each bus holds
    30 students. How many buses
    will they use?

_____   _____

Name _____

Choosing a Reasonable Scale

Vocabulary

Write the vocabulary word that best describes the part of a graph.

1. a series of numbers placed at fixed distances _____

2. the distance between each number on the scale _____

Choose the most reasonable interval for each set of data.

3. 25, 50, 70, 75, 100   4. 2, 4, 1, 7, 5   a. 25

_____   _____   b. 5

5. 5, 10, 30, 40, 20   6. 15, 25, 35, 20, 40   c. 10

_____   _____   d. 1

Circle the letter of the more reasonable scale for the set of data.

7.

FIFTH-GRADE SURVEY	
Favorite Color	Number of Students
Red	40
Blue	50
Green	20
Yellow	10
Other	10

a. 60 40 20 0   b. 50 40 30 20 10 0

8.

CAKE SALE	
Week	Number Sold
1	10
2	5
3	15
4	12
5	20

a. 25 20 15 10 5 0   b. 80 60 40 20 0

Mixed Applications

For Problems 9–10, use the table.

9. What would be an appropriate scale for these data?

_____

10. How many students were surveyed?

_____

SNACK SURVEY	
Favorite Snack	Number
Oatmeal cookies	18
Sandwich	20
Fruit	10

Making Line Graphs

Vocabulary

Complete.

1. The _____ is the difference between the greatest and least numbers in a set of data.

Make a line graph for each set of data.

2.

Books Read					
Week	1	2	3	4	5
Number of Books	15	10	20	10	5

3.

Inches of Snowfall					
Month	Nov	Dec	Jan	Feb	Mar
Inches	4	12	8	6	2

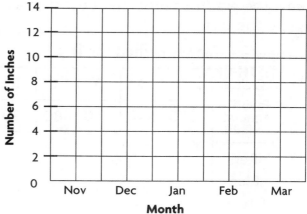

Mixed Applications

For Problems 4–5, use the table.

TIME SHEILA SPENDS PLAYING PIANO					
Day	**Mon**	**Tue**	**Wed**	**Thu**	**Fri**
Time	10 min	20 min	30 min	20 min	15 min

4. What would be an appropriate scale for a line graph displaying these data?

_____

5. What are the mean, median, and mode for the time Sheila spent playing the piano?

_____

Name _____

Choosing the Appropriate Graph

For Problems 1–4, choose a type of graph or plot. Explain your choice.

1. monthly high temperatures for a city over a 6-month period

_____

_____

2. heights of students in a class

_____

_____

3. most popular athletic shoe brand in a class

_____

_____

4. money spent on food each week over a 5-week period

_____

_____

Draw the graph or plot that best displays each set of data.

5.

Money Earned For Trip					
Week	1	2	3	4	5
Amount	$50	$40	$60	$80	$90

6.

Favorite TV Network					
	ABC	NBC	CBS	FOX	CNN
Sixth Graders	5	10	20	20	30
Third Graders	20	15	15	30	5

Mixed Applications

For Problems 7–9, use the table.

7. What type of graph would you use to display these data? Explain.

_____

8. What is the number of pets most students own?

_____

Pets Owned in Mr. Craig's Class						
Number of Pets	0	1	2	3	4	5
Number of Students	5	7	6	8	2	1

9. What is the total number of students surveyed?

_____

Problem-Solving Strategy

Make a Graph

Make a graph to solve.

1.

New Mascot		
Wolf	Bear	Lion
160	140	100

Mr. Brown, the principal, surveyed students to find out which mascot they wanted. He organized the data in a table. What graph or plot should he use to display these data? Make the graph or plot.

2.

Homework Pages Assigned					
Month	Sep	Oct	Nov	Dec	Jan
Number of Pages	40	60	80	40	80

Mr. Flores kept track of the number of homework pages assigned to the class for 5 months. He recorded the data in a table. What graph or plot should he use to display these data? Make the graph or plot.

Mixed Applications

Solve.

CHOOSE A STRATEGY

Make a Table • Make a Graph • Guess and Check • Write a Number Sentence

3. Ben sold newspaper subscriptions. He sold 20 subscriptions on Monday and on Tuesday, 15 subscriptions on Wednesday and Thursday, and 30 subscriptions on Friday. What is the mean number of subscriptions Ben sold?

_____

4. Samantha saved $35.50 to buy new clothes. She bought a shirt for $15.80 and a pair of pants for $12.75. How many pairs of socks priced at $1.99 a pair can she buy?

_____

5. A carton has a volume of 400 cu cm. Its length is 10 cm and its width is 5 cm. What is its height?

_____

6. Tracey has 4 coins in her pocket. If she has $0.46 in her pocket, what coins does she have?

_____

Reading Circle Graphs

Vocabulary

Complete.

1. A _____ shows data as parts of a whole circle.

For Problems 2–3, use the circle graph.

Grace's 60-Minute Workout

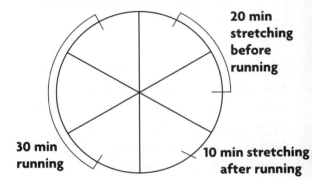

2. What does the whole circle represent?

_____

3. How many minutes did Grace spend stretching?

_____

Describe how the circle graph above would change for the data.

4. Grace spends 10 minutes stretching before and after running and 40 minutes running.

_____

_____

_____

5. Grace spends 10 minutes stretching before running, 30 minutes running and 20 minutes strength training after running.

_____

_____

_____

Mixed Applications

For Problem 6, use the circle graph.

6. What fraction of the time after school does Shawna spend on soccer? on TV? on dinner? on homework?

_____

Shawna's After-School Time

Making Circle Graphs

Use fraction-circle pieces to make a circle graph.

1.

GOALS SCORED BY HOCKEY TEAM		
Team Member	Number	Fraction of All Goals
Josh	4	$\frac{1}{4}$
Sara	4	$\frac{1}{4}$
Wiley	8	$\frac{1}{2}$

2.

BEV'S 60 CDS	
Type of CD	Fraction of All CDs
Classical	$\frac{1}{3}$
Rock	$\frac{1}{2}$
Jazz	$\frac{1}{6}$

3.

SID'S MONTHLY EXPENSES		
Items Purchased	Money Spent	Fraction of Total Spent
Snacks	$20	$\frac{1}{8}$
Hobbies	$20	$\frac{1}{8}$
Clothing	$60	$\frac{3}{8}$
Video games	$60	$\frac{3}{8}$

4.

WHAT SAM STUDIES IN 2 HOURS	
Subject	Fraction of Total Time
Science	$\frac{1}{4}$
Math	$\frac{3}{8}$
History	$\frac{1}{4}$
English	$\frac{1}{8}$

Mixed Applications

5. The yearbook staff sold 400 yearbooks at the beginning of the year and 80 yearbooks at the end of the year. If the books sold for $10 each, how much money did the yearbook staff collect?

_____

6. Craig invited 20 people to his party. He wants to give each person a bag with 8 balloons and 5 scratch-and-sniff pencils. How many balloons and pencils does he need to buy?

_____

7. Each yearbook has 16 pages. Paper for the yearbook is $0.07 a page. If 500 yearbooks were printed, what was the final cost for paper?

_____

8. Samuel read 18 books in June, July, and August. He read 4 books in August. He read three times that amount in June. How many books did he read in July?

_____

Decimals in Circle Graphs

For Problems 1–2, use the circle graph.

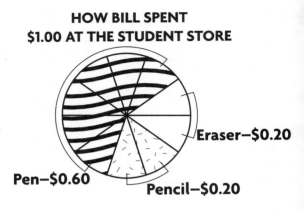

**HOW BILL SPENT
$1.00 AT THE STUDENT STORE**

Eraser—$0.20

Pen—$0.60

Pencil—$0.20

1. Bill spent $1.00 at the student store. What part of $1.00 did he spend for a pen and pencil?

_____

2. What fraction represents the part of the $1.00 that Bill spent for a pen? a pencil? an eraser?

_____

3. Make a circle graph for the data in the table.

SUE'S $1.00 SPENT AT THE STORE		
Item	Amount Spent	Decimal Part
Sourtarts	$0.50	0.5
Gumby Bears	$0.20	0.2
Licorice	$0.20	0.2
N and N's	$0.10	0.1

4. How would the circle graph change if Sue spent $1.00 on Sourtarts, $0.40 on Gumby Bears, $0.40 on Licorice, and $0.20 on N and N's?

_____

Mixed Applications

For Problems 5–6, use the circle graph.

FAVORITE SCIENCE TOPIC

Plants

Rocketry

Electricity

5. Write a decimal to represent the number of students out of 100 who said plants was their favorite science topic.

_____

6. Write a fraction to represent the number of students out of 100 who said rocketry was their favorite science topic.

_____

Analyzing Graphs

Explain why each graph does not correctly show the data.

1.

TOM'S BASEBALL CARD COLLECTION	
First Base	5 cards
Second Base	2 cards
Shortstop	1 card
Third Base	2 cards

TOM'S BASEBALL CARD COLLECTION

2.

GROWTH OF TOM'S BASEBALL CARD COLLECTION	
June	4 cards
July	6 cards
August	10 cards
September	12 cards

GROWTH OF TOM'S BASEBALL CARD COLLECTION

Mixed Applications

For Problems 3–5, use the circle graph.

3. What decimal represents the part of the $100 earned from ticket sales for miniature golf?

_____

4. What fraction represents the part of the $100 earned from ticket sales for the batting cage?

_____

$100 EARNED IN TICKET SALES FOR FAMILY NIGHT

$40–Miniature Golf

$10–Batting Cage

$50–Go Carts

5. If a game of miniature golf costs $2.50, how many people played miniature golf on Family Night?

_____

Comparing Graphs

Choose the best type of graph to display the data. Explain your choice.

1. amount of rainfall each month for a year in your state

_____

_____

2. how many newspapers were collected each week

_____

_____

3. the number of different types of cars on the road, such as mini-vans, sedans, wagons

_____

_____

4. how the Federal government spends each part of your tax dollar

_____

_____

5.

Monthly Sales Amounts	
Sep	$500,000
Oct	$600,000
Nov	$700,000
Dec	$900,000

_____

_____

6.

STUDENTS ON HONOR ROLL	
Grade	Number of Students
4th	48
5th	83
6th	64

_____

_____

Mixed Applications

For Problem 7, use the table.

7. What type of graph would best display these data? Explain.

_____

_____

Number of 100% Spelling Tests	
Week 1	12
Week 2	18
Week 3	20
Week 4	30

Name _____

Problem-Solving Strategy

Make a Graph

Choose the best type of graph to display the data. Then make the graph.

1. Mr. Jenning's fifth-grade class separated into three different groups to plan a party. Of the class, 0.7 worked on decorations, 0.2 worked on food, and 0.1 worked on music. What type of graph could you use to display these data?

_____

2. Mrs. Kent's fifth-grade class went on a field trip to the zoo. For the field trip 15 students brought cameras, 8 students brought video cameras, and 7 students brought neither. What graph could you use to display these data?

_____

Mixed Applications

Solve.

CHOOSE A STRATEGY

Guess and Check • Act It Out • Make a Graph • Work Backward • Make a Table • Draw a Diagram

3. Sid has $0.80 in nickels and quarters. He has a total of 8 coins, and the number of nickels is 4 more than the number of quarters. How many nickels and quarters does he have?

_____

4. The gym holds 30 rows of chairs with 28 chairs in each row. How many students can be seated in the gym?

_____

Certain, Impossible, Likely

Vocabulary

Fill in the blanks.

1. An event is _____ if it will always happen.

2. An event is _____ if it will never happen.

Write *certain* or *impossible* for each event.

3. that Earth rotates

_____

4. that there will be 2 Tuesdays next week

_____

5. rolling a 7 on a cube numbered 1–6

_____

6. that there are 13 months in a year

_____

7. that the sun will rise tomorrow morning

_____

8. pulling a blue counter from a bag containing six blue counters

_____

Write whether each event is *likely* or *unlikely*.

9. rain falling in Seattle in winter

_____

10. the cafeteria serving octopus

_____

11. tossing a coin 100 times and getting heads at least 10 times

_____

12. pulling the winning number out of a hat filled with 50 numbers

_____

Mixed Applications

13. Patti has 6 blue bows and 1 red bow in a box. She picks 1 without looking. Is it certain or likely that she will pick a blue bow?

_____

14. A magazine that costs $2.50 a month on the newsstand offers a 1-year subscription for $19.95. How much is saved by getting a subscription?

_____

Probability Experiments

Vocabulary

Fill in the blank.

1. A table of _____ shows
results that could occur.

For Problems 2–4, use a spinner with six sections
labeled 1, 1, 1, 2, 2, 3.

2. In the table at the right, list the possible
outcomes.

3. Predict and record the number of times
you think each outcome will occur if you
spin 20 times.

Spinner Experiment			
Possible outcomes			
Predicted frequency			
Actual frequency			

_____

_____

4. Spin 20 times. Record the results in the
table.

For Problems 5–6, use the table.

5. Why do you think you spin 1 so
often?

_____

6. Which number has a higher
actual frequency, 2 or 3?

_____

Mixed Applications

7. Chantal has a spinner divided
into 4 equal sections. There are
blue, red, green, and yellow
sections. If she spins 10 times,
what are the possible outcomes?

_____

8. Marland collects cards and stores
them in plastic sheets. Each sheet
holds 12 cards. If Marland has
46 full sheets, how many cards
does he have?

_____

Recording Outcomes in Tree Diagrams

Vocabulary

Fill in the blank.

1. A _____ shows all the possible outcomes of an event.

Complete the tree diagram. Tell the number of choices.

Dessert	Flavors	Choices
	chocolate chip	chocolate chip cookies
2. cookies	_____	peanut butter cookies
	oatmeal	_____
	_____	chocolate cake
3. cake	vanilla	_____
	_____	strawberry cake

4. number of dessert choices: _____

Find the number of choices by making a tree diagram.

5.

Music Choices			
Format	CD	video	tape
Type	rock	classical	jazz

number of choices: _____

6.

Book Selections		
Type	mystery	science fiction
Format	hard cover	paperback

number of choices: _____

Mixed Applications

7. Kyle wants to buy earrings for Tanya. He can buy hoop, stud, or drop earrings in gold or silver. How many choices does he have?

_____

8. Joanne has $0.40 more than Cory. Together they have $9.30. How much money does each girl have?

_____

_____

Problem-Solving Strategy

Make an Organized List

Make an organized list to solve.

1. Aber is conducting a probability experiment with a number cube and two marbles. The cube is numbered 1–6. One marble is red, the other blue. How many possible outcomes are there for this experiment? What are they?

   _____

   _____

   _____

   _____

2. Mark feeds his cat a cup of dry food and a can of wet food every day. The dry food is either chicken or fish flavored. The wet food is either tuna, salmon, or beef. List all the possible combinations of wet and dry cat food.

   _____

   _____

   _____

   _____

Mixed Applications

Solve.

CHOOSE A STRATEGY

• **Make an Organized List** • **Make a Graph** • **Work Backward** • **Act It Out** • **Guess and Check**

3. In the school election, Dave received 38 percent of the vote, Marcia received 41 percent, and Claudia received 21 percent. What type of graph would Dave use to display the data?

   _____

4. Estelle uses the numbers 3, 5, and 7 to write two-digit numbers without repeating any digits in the same number. List her numbers.

   _____

5. Martha has 6 coins that are quarters, dimes, and nickels. She has a total of $0.80. What combination of coins does she have?

   _____

6. At the movies, Jorge spent $0.95 on soda and $2.25 on popcorn. The ticket cost $4.50. If he has $2.30 left, how much money did Jorge have to begin with?

   _____

Finding Probability

Vocabulary

Fill in the blanks.

1. _____ is the chance that an event will happen.

2. Each outcome is _____, or has the same chance of happening.

Write a fraction for the probability of pulling each color marble from a bag of 4 red, 1 green, 2 blue, and 3 yellow marbles.

3. green   4. red   5. orange   6. blue

_____   _____   _____   _____

Write a fraction for the probability of spinning each color on a spinner with 2 red, 3 yellow, 2 green, and 1 blue sections.

7. yellow   8. red   9. yellow or blue   10. blue

_____   _____   _____   _____

Mixed Applications

11. Angie is one of 30 girls trying out for the 12 positions on the basketball team. What is the probability that Angie will make the team?

_____

_____

12. Of 100 tickets available for the school raffle, Tom bought 3, Jack bought 5, and Mark bought 2. What is the probability of each boy winning?

_____

_____

Comparing Probabilities

For Problems 1–6, you have a bag of 3 red, 5 blue, 4 yellow,
and 3 green buttons. Write each probability as a fraction.
Tell which outcome is more likely.

1. You pull a yellow button. ———

   You pull a red button. ———

   More likely _____

2. You pull a blue button. ———

   You pull a green button. ———

   More likely _____

3. You pull a red or yellow button.

   ———

   You pull a green or blue button.

   ———

   More likely _____

4. You pull a blue button.

   ———

   You pull a black button.

   ———

   More likely _____

5. You pull a button that isn't

   green. ———

   You pull a button that isn't

   yellow. ———

   More likely _____

6. You pull a button that isn't red.

   ———

   You pull a button that isn't blue.

   ———

   More likely _____

Mixed Applications

7. Joey had 2 pairs of red socks, 4
   pairs of black socks, and 12 pairs
   of white socks. What is the probability that he will pull a pair of
   black socks from his drawer?

   _____

8. Raimondo has pizza once a week
   for dinner. What is the probability
   that he will have pizza for dinner
   tonight?

   _____

Multiplying Decimals and Whole Numbers

Make a model to find each product.

1. $2 \times 0.5 = n$ **2.** $3 \times 0.4 = n$ **3.** $2 \times 0.25 = n$ **4.** $0.17 \times 3 = n$

_____   _____   _____   _____

5. $4 \times 0.7 = n$ **6.** $0.11 \times 4 = n$ **7.** $3 \times 0.8 = n$ **8.** $0.33 \times 2 = n$

_____   _____   _____   _____

Phillip is buying school supplies at the student book store.
For Problems 9–13, use the pictures.

9. 2 pencils, 2 erasers

_____

10. 2 markers, 1 protractor

_____

11. 3 pencils, 2 compasses

_____

12. 4 markers, 2 erasers, 1 protractor

_____

13. 3 compasses, 2 markers, 1 pencil

_____

Mixed Applications

14. Phyllis is shopping at the student
book store. Which costs more—
2 markers, or 1 compass and
2 pencils?

_____

15. Sam has $0.36. He has
5 coins. What are they?

_____

Name _____

Patterns in Decimal Factors and Products

Record the decimal multiplication sentences for each.

1.

Ones	Tenths	Hundredths

2.

Ones	Tenths	Hundredths

Draw models to find each product.

3. $2 \times 2 =$ _____

$2 \times 0.2 =$ _____

$2 \times 0.02 =$ _____

4. $2 \times 5 =$ _____

$2 \times 0.5 =$ _____

$2 \times 0.05 =$ _____

Use mental math to complete the pattern.

5. $1 \times 7 = 7$

$0.1 \times 7 = 0.7$

$0.01 \times 7 =$ _____

6. $1 \times 12 = 12$

$0.1 \times 12 =$ _____

$0.01 \times 12 = 0.12$

7. $1 \times 23 = 23$

$0.1 \times 23 =$ _____

$0.01 \times 23 =$ _____

8. $1 \times 35 = 35$

$0.1 \times 35 =$ _____

$0.01 \times 35 =$ _____

Mixed Applications

9. A penny is 0.01 of a dollar. There are 50 pennies in a roll. How much is 3 rolls of pennies?

_____

_____

10. A dime is 0.10 of a dollar. There are 50 dimes in a roll. How much is 2 rolls of dimes?

_____

_____

Multiplying a Decimal by a Decimal

Complete the multiplication number sentence for each drawing.

1.

2.

3.

4.

$0.3 \times 0.4 = n$ $\underline{\text{n}} \times 0.7 = 0.28$ $\underline{\text{n}} \times 0.8 = 0.16$ $0.7 \times \underline{\text{n}} = 0.42$

_____   _____   _____   _____

Multiply. Write each product.

5. $0.6 \times 0.3 =$ _____   6. $0.4 \times 0.2 =$ _____   7. $0.7 \times 0.7 =$ _____

8. $0.7 \times 0.6 =$ _____   9. $0.4 \times 0.9 =$ _____   10. $0.9 \times 0.3 =$ _____

11. $0.8 \times 0.6 =$ _____   12. $0.2 \times 0.5 =$ _____   13. $0.5 \times 0.3 =$ _____

14. $0.8 \times 0.5 =$ _____   15. $0.1 \times 0.9 =$ _____   16. $0.4 \times 0.4 =$ _____

17. $0.7 \times 0.5 =$ _____   18. $0.2 \times 0.6 =$ _____   19. $0.6 \times 0.6 =$ _____

20. $0.5 \times 0.4 =$ _____   21. $0.8 \times 0.7 =$ _____   22. $0.9 \times 0.5 =$ _____

Mixed Applications

23. Suppose you may eat 0.2 of the 0.5 cake that is left. How much can you eat?

_____

24. Frank earns $4.67 each day at his job. How much does he earn in 100 days?

_____

25. You order a giant cookie. Suppose you want 0.4 of the cookie to be covered with red sprinkles. If you want 0.5 of the sprinkled area also to have icing, how much of the cookie will have icing and sprinkles?

_____

26. Susan bought note cards. She paid $2.00 for a set of 5 cards and $0.40 for each additional card. How much will Susan pay for 11 cards?

_____

Problem-Solving Strategy

Make a Model

Make a model to solve.

1. Mary has 16 ft of trim to use as a border on a blanket. She wants to make a rectangular blanket with the greatest possible area. What dimensions should the border have?

   _____

   _____

2. Sam sells school spirit stickers. He collects $1.70 in coins. If he has 4 quarters, two more dimes than quarters, and the rest in nickels, how much of each coin does he have?

   _____

   _____

3. If 1 person can sit on each side of a square table, how many people can sit at 3 tables that are pushed together end to end to form a rectangle?

   _____

4. Five friends are standing in line. Henry and Fred are next to each other and are between Lisa and John. Lisa is next to Henry. Fred and Mary are standing beside each other. Who is next to John?

   _____

Mixed Applications

Solve.

┌─────────── CHOOSE A STRATEGY ───────────┐

• **Work Backward**   • **Make a Table**   • **Find a Pattern**   • **Make a Model**

5. The product of two decimal numbers is 0.10. One number is 0.3 more than the other number. What are the two numbers?

   _____

6. Marsha has 200 flyers to hand out. If she can hand out 50 flyers in 20 minutes, how long will it take her to hand out all of the flyers?

   _____

7. Shirley buys a package of apples that weighs 3 pounds and costs $0.85 per pound. How much change will she receive from $5.00?

   _____

   _____

8. Todd earns $59.50 per week for 5 weeks. He puts $10.00 a week in his savings account. How much does he keep to spend?

   _____

   _____

Placing the Decimal Point

Vocabulary

1. What is the place value of 5 in the number 7.8645?

_____

Choose the best estimate. Write *a*, *b*, or *c*.

2. $11 \times 0.3 = n$ _____ a. 3 b. 30 c. 300

3. $24 \times 0.6 = n$ _____ a. 1.2 b. 12 c. 120

4. $42 \times 0.9 = n$ _____ a. 4 b. 40 c. 60

5. $36 \times 0.4 = n$ _____ a. 0.9 b. 6 c. 15

6. $\$0.83 \times 2 = n$ _____ a. \$1.60 b. \$16.00 c. \$160.00

7. $\$0.43 \times 5 = n$ _____ a. \$0.20 b. \$2.00 c. \$4.00

Use estimation and patterns to place the decimal point in
each product.

8. $2.3 \times 7 = 161$ 9. $2.3 \times 0.7 = 161$ 10. $23 \times 0.7 = 161$

_____ _____ _____

11. $0.23 \times 0.7 = 161$ 12. $23 \times 7 = 161$ 13. $0.23 \times 7 = 161$

_____ _____ _____

14. $2.3 \times 0.07 = 161$ 15. $23 \times 0.007 = 161$ 16. $0.23 \times 0.07 = 161$

_____ _____ _____

Mixed Applications

17. Grace earns \$11.85 a week
babysitting. About how much
money does she earn in
12 weeks?

18. There is a total of 360 pieces in
Hector's dinosaur puzzle. If he
puts together 147 puzzle pieces,
how many pieces are left to
finish the puzzle?

_____ _____

More About Placing the Decimal Point

Estimate each product.

1. 6×0.21 **2.** 7×0.41 **3.** 0.23×95 **4.** 64×0.4

_____   _____   _____   _____

5. 0.64×9 **6.** 32×0.04 **7.** 0.98×46 **8.** 82×0.2

_____   _____   _____   _____

9. Complete the table.

Number Sentence	Factors	Products
$0.3 \times 0.6 = 0.18$	tenths $\times$ tenths	_____
$0.3 \times$ _____ $= 0.018$	tenths $\times$ _____	_____
_____ $\times$ _____ $= 0.0018$	_____	_____
_____ $\times 0.006 =$ _____	_____	_____

Estimate to place the decimal point. Then find the product.

10. $\$3.50 \times 2 = n$ **11.** $2.1 \times 14 = n$ **12.** $0.8 \times 6.7 = n$ **13.** $1.15 \times 49 = n$

_____   _____   _____   _____

14. $\$6.30$
   $\times 7$
    _____

15. 0.27
   $\times 0.3$
    _____

16. 0.82
   $\times 13$
    _____

17. $\$1.19$
   $\times 97$
    _____

_____   _____   _____   _____

Mixed Applications

18. Samuel buys a gallon of milk at $\$1.29$ and 2 dozen pretzels at $\$2.19$ a dozen. About how much does he spend?

19. John chooses a present for his father that costs $\$13.95$. He gives the cashier $\$20.00$. How much change will he receive?

_____   _____

Multiplying Mixed Decimals

Vocabulary

Complete.

1. A _____ has a whole-number part and a
   decimal part in the number.

Find the product.

2.	2.84	3.	21.6	4.	$73.49	5.	345.2	6.	401.23
	× 3.4		× 0.52		× 5.7		× 0.13		× 3.6

7.	23.7	8.	56.1	9.	$9.62	10.	62.4	11.	2.004
	× 4.02		× 3.8		× 1.5		× 3.05		× 2.2

12. $1.8 \times 2.4 =$ _____   13. $1.2 \times 1.3 =$ _____   14. $2.2 \times 2.3 =$ _____

Solve. For Problems 15–16, use the table.

15. How much are 2 pairs of low top
    tennis shoes at Stand Up?

    _____

16. What is the total cost of 2 pairs of
    high top tennis shoes at Shoeland,
    including a sales tax of $0.06 on
    each dollar?

    _____

SHOE STORE PRICES		
Store	**Low Tops**	**High Tops**
Shoes-R-US	$24.25	$33.50
Shoeland	$22.50	$35.75
Stand Up	$28.75	$39.75
Running Fast	$21.25	$34.50

Mixed Applications

17. Samuel bought a pen for $0.87. If
    he paid a sales tax of $0.06, what
    did he spend on the pen?

    _____

18. Susan was billed $1.20 for a
    phone call. The phone company
    charges $0.40 for the first minute
    and $0.10 for each additional
    minute. How long did she talk?

    _____

Patterns in Decimal Division

Complete each pattern.

1. $600 \div 4 =$ _____

   $60 \div 4 =$ _____

   $6 \div 4 =$ _____

2. $100 \div 5 =$ _____

   $10 \div 5 =$ _____

   $1 \div 5 =$ _____

3. $200 \div 5 =$ _____

   $20 \div 5 =$ _____

   $2 \div 5 =$ _____

4. $300 \div 6 =$ _____

   $30 \div 6 =$ _____

   $3 \div 6 =$ _____

5. $500 \div 4 =$ _____

   $50 \div 4 =$ _____

   $5 \div 4 =$ _____

6. $1,200 \div 8 =$ _____

   $120 \div 8 =$ _____

   $12 \div 8 =$ _____

7. $100 \div 4 =$ _____

   $10 \div 4 =$ _____

   $1 \div 4 =$ _____

8. $1,400 \div 5 =$ _____

   $140 \div 5 =$ _____

   $14 \div 5 =$ _____

9. $1,000 \div 4 =$ _____

   $100 \div 4 =$ _____

   $10 \div 4 =$ _____

Mixed Applications

10. Phil saves 1,183 pennies. How much money does he have in dollars and cents?

_____

11. Sid earns $60 dollars a week. He works 5 hours each week. How much does he earn per hour?

_____

12. Theresa has 120 bows to make. She can make 6 bows in 10 minutes. How long will it take her to make all of the bows?

_____

13. Harry needs $160 to buy a bike. He has $70. If he saves $10 each week, how many weeks will it take to save enough to buy the bike?

_____

14. Chantel recorded in the table at the right the amount of money she spent on lunch at school for a week. On which day did she spend the most money? the least money?

_____

Day	Amount
Monday	$2.25
Tuesday	$3.65
Wednesday	$2.05
Thursday	$1.25
Friday	$3.50

Problem-Solving Strategy

Write a Number Sentence

Write a number sentence to solve.

1. Sam and 4 classmates buy a present for their teacher. The bill for the present is $30. They share the bill equally. How much does each owe?

2. Samantha has saved $600 in her savings account. She made 10 equal deposits. How much was each deposit?

3. Each day Sam makes $8 from his dog-walking business. In 12 days, how much money will he make?

4. Cherie and Phillip worked together on a school project. Cherie spent $3.25 on supplies. Phillip spent $4.50. How much money did they spend in all?

Mixed Applications

Solve.

CHOOSE A STRATEGY

- **Make a Table**
- **Guess and Check**
- **Write a Number Sentence**

5. Henry wants to buy 6 basketball cards. At Sam's Trading Post 1 basketball card sells for $1.25. At Carl's Card Shop a set of 3 basketball cards sells for $3.60. Which store offers the better buy?

6. John wants to buy 2 new CDs. At Computers-R-Us, the CDs are 2 for $25.00. At Computerville, they are $11.95 each. What is the difference in the price for one CD?

7. Cynthia has 875 pennies and her sister Connie has 458 pennies. If the number of pennies doubles each year, how many pennies will they have in all after 2 years?

8. Sid mailed a letter. It weighed 3 ounces. The cost to mail it is 32¢ for the first ounce and 12¢ for each additional ounce. What is the cost of the letter?

Decimal Division

Make a model and find the quotient.

1. $1.8 \div 2 =$ _____

2. $2.4 \div 6 =$ _____

3. $0.25 \div 5 =$ _____

4. $0.48 \div 4 =$ _____

Use the model to complete the number sentence.

5.

$2.8 \div 4 =$ _____

Mixed Applications

6. Sam wants to decorate 4 presents. He has ribbon that is 3.2 meters long. How long will each ribbon be if he divides the ribbon evenly among the 4 presents?

_____

7. Marcia is making a quilt that is 4.5 feet × 6.5 feet. What is the area of Marcia's quilt?

_____

Dividing Decimals by Whole Numbers

Find the quotient. Check by multiplying.

1. $8\overline{)4.8}$ $\times \quad 8$ 2. $4\overline{)2.24}$ $\times \quad 4$ 3. $6\overline{)4.98}$ $\times \quad 6$

4. $7\overline{)47.6}$ $\times \quad 7$ 5. $2\overline{)6.06}$ $\times \quad 2$ 6. $3\overline{)2.22}$ $\times \quad 3$

7. $5\overline{)6.15}$ $\times \quad 5$ 8. $2\overline{)16.8}$ $\times \quad 2$ 9. $6\overline{)8.1}$ $\times \quad 6$

10.

$22.4 \div 7 = \underline{\ ?\ }$ $\times \quad 7$

11.

$2.24 \div 7 = \underline{\ ?\ }$ $\times \quad 7$

12.

$0.63 \div 3 = \underline{\ ?\ }$ $\times \quad 3$

Mixed Applications

13. At the local Farmer's Market, oranges cost $6.75 for 5 pounds. How much does 1 pound cost?

14. Sara is finishing her curtains. She buys 2 pieces of lace to edge the bottom. The 2 pieces cost $6.84. How much does each piece cost?

_____

_____

Placing the Decimal Point

Use estimation or patterns to place the decimal point. Then find the quotient.

1. 4)2.8

2. 5)4.5

3. 8)0.24

4. 2)0.04

5. 3)4.8

6. 6)10.2

7. 8)29.6

8. 9)48.6

9. 7)9.38

10. 4)11.04

11. 5)15.45

12. 4)21.52

Mixed Applications

For Problems 13–15, use the price list.

13. Sunder bought a package of hot dogs and two packages of hot dog buns. How much did he spend?

_____

14. Estimate the cost of 1 pound of apples.

_____

THIS WEEK'S
SuperSaver Specials

Apples 3 lb. bag   **$3.27**
Juice boxes 6 pk   **$2.56**
Juice box single   75¢
Hot Dogs 8 pk   **$1.58**
Hot Dog Buns 8 pk 68¢

15. What is the cost of 3 packs of juice boxes?

_____

Choosing the Operation

For Problems 1–4, use the table. Choose the operation and solve.

1. Sara buys some beans and shares each kind of bean equally with her 2 neighbors. How many pounds of garbanzo beans does Sara have after sharing with her neighbors?

Type of Beans	Amount (in pounds)
Garbanzo beans	22.5
Black beans	64.2
Pinto beans	13.5

_____

2. How many pounds of black beans does Sara have after sharing with her neighbors?

_____

3. How many pounds of pinto beans does Sara have after sharing with her neighbors?

_____

4. How many pounds of beans does Sara buy in all?

_____

5. Sara buys 6.4 pounds of rice each week for 4 weeks. How many pounds of rice does Sara buy?

_____

Mixed Applications

6. Grant is comparing shampoos. Brand A weighs 10 ounces and sells for $3.52. Brand B weighs 8 ounces and sells for $2.16. Which shampoo costs less per ounce?

_____

7. Donald bought 3 baseballs for $4.58 each, a baseball bat for $18.79, and a baseball glove for $23.52. How much did all of these items cost?

_____

8. The Feldman School bought $962.50 worth of football tickets. The tickets cost $28.50 apiece. Estimate how many tickets were purchased.

_____

9. Championship football tickets sold out quickly. In $1\frac{1}{2}$ hours all 6,000 tickets were sold. Estimate how many tickets were sold each minute.

_____

Linear Units

Vocabulary

Write the correct letter from Column 2.

Column 1   Column 2

1. _____ millimeter(s) (mm) = 1 meter (m)   **a.** 100

2. _____ centimeter(s) (cm) = 1 meter (m)   **b.** 1

3. _____ decimeter(s) (dm) = 1 meter (m)   **c.** 1,000

4. _____ kilometer(s) (km) = 1,000 meters (m)   **d.** 10

Choose the most reasonable unit of measure. Write *mm, cm, dm, m,* or *km.*

5. length of your classroom   **6.** thickness of a CD

_____   _____

7. height of a portable TV   **8.** thickness of a glass window

_____   _____

9. length of a marathon   **10.** length of a dollar bill

_____   _____

Write the measurements in order from shortest to longest.

11. 2 km, 2 dm, 2 mm   **12.** 6 m, 6 mm, 6 dm

_____   _____

13. 72 dm, 72 m, 72 cm   **14.** 18 m, 18 km, 18 mm

_____   _____

Mixed Applications

15. Chantal ran in a 3,000-meter race. How many kilometers did Chantal run?

_____

16. Greg's room has a width of 3 m and a length of 4 m. Would a 150-dm border be long enough to fit around the room's perimeter?

_____

Units of Mass

Vocabulary

Fill in the blanks.

1. 1 gram (g) = _____ milligrams (mg)

2. 1 kilogram (kg) = _____ grams (g)

Choose the most reasonable unit. Write *kg, g,* or *mg*.

3. a person

_____

4. a T-shirt

_____

5. a hamburger

_____

6. a stamp

_____

7. a surfboard

_____

8. a scarf

_____

Choose the more reasonable measurement.

9.

500 mg or 500 g

_____

10.

150 mg or 150 g

_____

11.

1g or 1 kg

_____

12.

15 kg or 15 g

_____

13.

250 g or 250 mg

_____

14.

60 g or 60 kg

_____

Mixed Applications

15. A serving of tortilla chips contains 140 mg of salt. How many mg of salt are in 8 servings of tortilla chips?

_____

16. One g of fat equals 9 calories. How many calories are from fat if a 175-calorie muffin has 5 g of fat

_____

Units of Capacity and Volume

Vocabulary

Complete.

1. The _____ of a container measures the amount the container will hold.

2. 1,000 _____ = 1 liter

3. 1 _____ = 4 metric cups

4. 1,000 liters = 1 _____

Choose the reasonable unit. Write *mL, L,* or *kL.*

5.

6.

7.

_____   _____   _____

Choose the more reasonable measurement.

8.

9.

10.

473 mL or 473 L   4 L or 4 kL   651 mL or 651 L

_____   _____   _____

Mixed Applications

11. A storage shed is 14 ft long, 12 ft wide, and 10 ft high. What is the volume of the storage shed?

12. Aber uses 35 L of water to give her dog a bath. How many mL of water does Aber use?

_____   _____

Relating Metric Units

Vocabulary

Match the prefix in Column 2 with the base unit in Column 1.

Column 1   Column 2

1. _____ hundredths   **a.** deci-

2. _____ tenths   **b.** milli-

3. _____ thousands   **c.** centi-

4. _____ thousandths   **d.** kilo-

Choose the smaller unit of measure. Write *a* or *b*. Use the prefix to help you.

5. **a.** milliliter _____   6. **a.** decimeter _____   7. **a.** gram _____

    b. kiloliter   **b.** centimeter   **b.** kilogram

Choose the larger unit of measure. Write *a* or *b*.

8. **a.** liter _____   9. **a.** gram _____   10. **a.** centimeter _____

    b. kiloliter   **b.** milligram   **b.** millimeter

Write the equivalent measurement.

11. 900 millimeters = _____ meter   12. 0.6 meter = _____ centimeters

13. 4,500 milligrams = _____ gram   14. 3 kiloliters = _____ liters

15. 30 milliliters = _____ liter   16. 7 grams = _____ milligrams

Mixed Applications

17. There are 25 students in Emma's class. She wants to get enough juice to serve each student 300 mL. How many liters of juice does Emma need?

18. Sharon ran a 10-km race last weekend. Peter ran a 1,000-m race the same day. Who ran the longer race?

_____   _____

Name _____

Changing Units

Write the missing unit.

1. 3 km = 3,000 _____   **2.** 6 L = 6,000 _____

3. 400 cm = 40 _____   **4.** 1.5 kg = 1,500 _____

5. 43.5 dm = 4.35 _____   **6.** 555 mm = 5.55 _____

7. 0.8 kL = 800 _____   **8.** 2 m = 200 _____

Write *multiply* or *divide*. Then write the equivalent measurement.

9. 3.5 m = $\frac{?}{}$ cm   **10.** 200 mL = $\frac{?}{}$ L

_____   _____

11. 9 L = $\frac{?}{}$ mL   **12.** 7 kg = $\frac{?}{}$ g

_____   _____

13. 6.4 g = $\frac{?}{}$ mg   **14.** 500 mm = $\frac{?}{}$ dm

_____   _____

15. 4,400 g = $\frac{?}{}$ kg   **16.** 800 dm = $\frac{?}{}$ m

_____   _____

17. 30 cm = $\frac{?}{}$ dm   **18.** 7.5 m = $\frac{?}{}$ cm

_____   _____

Mixed Applications

19. Joanne has a backpack that weighs 0.78 kg. Debby's backpack weighs 775 grams. Who has the lighter backpack?

20. Evan said that he walked 1,000,000 centimeters on Saturday. How far did Evan walk in meters

_____   _____

21. Tim weighs his suitcase. Would the weight be 12 g or 12 kg?

22. Teresa earned $178 in 6 weeks. About how much did she earn each week?

_____   _____

Problem-Solving Strategy

Draw a Diagram

Draw a diagram to solve

1. Al noticed that his cereal box has a mass of 212.5 g. A serving size is 25 g. If Al eats 1 serving of cereal every day for 2 weeks, how many boxes of cereal will he need to buy?

_____

2. Gabrielle filled her 2 L water bottle. She drank 500 mL of water before her workout and 750 mL of water after her workout. How many liters of water are left in Gabrielle's bottle?

_____

3. A classroom table is 1 m wide and 1.75 m long. How many 39 cm wide chairs can fit around the table?

_____

4. Anna ran a marathon race, which is 42.19 km long. About how many 10,000 meter races equal the length of a marathon?

_____

Mixed Applications

Solve.

CHOOSE A STRATEGY

• Guess and Check • Make an Organized List • Work Backward • Write a Number Sentence • Find a Pattern

5. Janice spent $3 for a magazine. She spent half her remaining money on school supplies. Then she spent half her remaining money on a present. She had $8 remaining. How much money did Janice begin with?

_____

6. Anna walked 20 min her first day at the gym. The second day she walked 23 min. The third day she walked 26 min. If Anna continues to progress at the same rate how many minutes will she be able to walk on the twentieth day?

7. Egyptian surveyors used the knotted rope shown to make a right angle corner. Show how you could peg the rope to make a right triangle?

Understanding Fractions

Write the fraction shown.

1.

_____

2.

_____

3.

_____

4.

_____

5.

_____

6.

_____

Shade a fraction strip to show the fraction.

7. $\frac{1}{7}$ **8.** $\frac{4}{6}$ **9.** $\frac{5}{8}$

Draw a number line. Locate the fraction.

10. $\frac{2}{5}$ **11.** $\frac{7}{8}$ **12.** $\frac{2}{6}$

Mixed Applications

13. James has a bookcase with 6 shelves. He uses 4 of the shelves to store his books. What fraction of the shelves are not being used to store books?

_____

14. Miki plans to make a sash 45 cm long and a hair band 35 cm long. She has 8 dm of ribbon. Does she have enough ribbon? Explain.

_____

_____

Mixed Numbers

Vocabulary

Complete.

1. A _____ is made up of a whole
   number and a fraction.

For Problems 2–5, use the figures at the right.

2. How many whole figures are
   shaded?

   _____

3. Into how many parts is each figure
   divided?

   _____

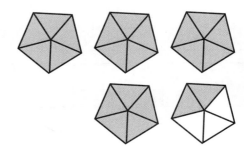

4. How many parts of the fifth figure
   are shaded?

   _____

5. Write a fraction and a mixed
   number for the figures.

   _____

Rename each fraction as a mixed number.

6. $\frac{22}{7}$ _____   7. $\frac{7}{5}$ _____   8. $\frac{19}{4}$ _____   9. $\frac{13}{2}$ _____

Rename each mixed number as a fraction.

10. $4\frac{2}{3}$ _____   11. $1\frac{4}{6}$ _____   12. $3\frac{2}{5}$ _____   13. $2\frac{2}{4}$ _____

Mixed Applications

14. Sam was asked to change $\frac{11}{3}$ to
    a mixed number, and $8\frac{1}{3}$ to a
    fraction. What answers should
    Sam give?

    _____

15. Maria takes 6 classes. In 5 of
    those classes, she has an A. Write
    a fraction to describe the fraction
    of classes in which she has an A.

    _____

Multiples and Least Common Multiples

Vocabulary

Complete.

1. The product of two or more numbers is a _____.

2. Multiples of one number that are also multiples of another

   number are called _____.

3. The smallest number that is a common multiple is called the

   _____, or _____.

Use counters to name the least common multiple for each.

4. 3 and 4   **5.** 2 and 6   **6.** 4 and 5   **7.** 8 and 6   **8.** 3 and 7

_____   _____   _____   _____   _____

Rename each pair of fractions so they have the same denominator.
Use counters and LCMs from Exercises 4–8.

9. $\frac{1}{3}$ and $\frac{1}{4}$ **10.** $\frac{1}{2}$ and $\frac{2}{6}$ **11.** $\frac{3}{4}$ and $\frac{2}{5}$

_____   _____   _____

12. $\frac{3}{8}$ and $\frac{5}{6}$ **13.** $\frac{2}{3}$ and $\frac{6}{7}$ **14.** $\frac{5}{6}$ and $\frac{1}{4}$

_____   _____   _____

Mixed Applications

15. Max uses $\frac{7}{12}$ of a bag of toothpicks to make a project. Tracy uses $\frac{5}{8}$ of a bag for her project. Rename the amount of bags that Max and Tracy use so that the fractions have the same denominator.

16. Janet is planting a garden. She wants to put a fence around it to keep the rabbits out. If the garden is 3 meters wide and 6.5 meters long, how much fencing does she need?

_____   _____

Comparing

Rename, using the least common multiple; then compare.
Write $<$, $>$, or $=$ in each $\bigcirc$.

1. $\frac{3}{12} \bigcirc \frac{5}{8}$ 2. $\frac{2}{8} \bigcirc \frac{7}{32}$ 3. $\frac{6}{8} \bigcirc \frac{3}{9}$ 4. $\frac{2}{3} \bigcirc \frac{6}{9}$

5. $\frac{5}{6} \bigcirc \frac{3}{4}$ 6. $\frac{3}{15} \bigcirc \frac{1}{3}$ 7. $\frac{6}{22} \bigcirc \frac{3}{11}$ 8. $\frac{3}{7} \bigcirc \frac{6}{21}$

9. $\frac{5}{6} \bigcirc \frac{5}{8}$ 10. $\frac{3}{7} \bigcirc \frac{11}{14}$ 11. $\frac{7}{12} \bigcirc \frac{3}{8}$ 12. $\frac{9}{10} \bigcirc \frac{6}{7}$

13. $\frac{12}{40} \bigcirc \frac{6}{10}$ 14. $\frac{4}{5} \bigcirc \frac{2}{4}$ 15. $\frac{4}{7} \bigcirc \frac{1}{2}$ 16. $\frac{3}{4} \bigcirc \frac{8}{9}$

Mixed Applications

17. Jacqueline is going to visit her relatives, who live 958.6 km away. On Monday, she drives 343.7 km. She drives 272.4 km on Tuesday and on Wednesday. How far must she drive on Thursday?

18. Every week Shelby takes a math quiz. The first week she got 17 correct. Then for the next four weeks, she got 6 more correct than on the previous week's quiz. How many questions did she get correct on her last quiz?

19. Doug painted $\frac{3}{5}$ of a design blue. He painted $\frac{6}{15}$ of it green. Which color is used more in his design?

20. If Nathan buys 3 books at $3.95 each and 2 magazines at $2.75 each, how much change will he receive if he gives the cashier $20?

21. Petra loves animals. She has twelve pets in all, four of which are rabbits. Write a fraction to describe the number of rabbits she has.

22. Flora's Flowers sells 3 roses for $13.50. The Green Thumb sells 4 roses for $15.00. Discount Flowers sells 6 roses for $23.00. Who sells roses at the lowest price?

Ordering

Rename the fractions, using the LCM as the denominator.

1. $\frac{1}{3}, \frac{1}{4}, \frac{1}{5}$

2. $\frac{5}{6}, \frac{3}{4}, \frac{5}{8}$

3. $\frac{2}{5}, \frac{1}{3}, \frac{3}{5}$

_____   _____   _____

4. $\frac{1}{6}, \frac{1}{9}, \frac{1}{3}$

5. $\frac{1}{2}, \frac{3}{8}, \frac{5}{12}$

6. $\frac{3}{4}, \frac{5}{8}, \frac{2}{3}$

_____   _____   _____

Write in order from least to greatest.

7. $\frac{2}{5}, \frac{2}{3}, \frac{4}{15}$

8. $\frac{2}{3}, \frac{3}{4}, \frac{7}{12}$

9. $\frac{7}{9}, \frac{1}{2}, \frac{11}{18}$

_____   _____   _____

Write in order from greatest to least.

10. $\frac{5}{6}, \frac{1}{4}, \frac{5}{12}$

11. $\frac{4}{5}, \frac{7}{10}, \frac{1}{2}$

12. $\frac{9}{15}, \frac{2}{3}, \frac{2}{5}$

_____   _____   _____

Mixed Applications

13. Gilbert is making snack mix for a school field trip. He uses $\frac{1}{2}$ cup dried apricots, $\frac{3}{5}$ cup peanuts, and $\frac{4}{7}$ cup raisins. List the ingredients in order from least to greatest.

14. Marisa wants to buy 1 pound of walnuts and $\frac{1}{2}$ pound of almonds. She has $12.00. If $\frac{1}{4}$ pound almonds costs $2.25 and $\frac{1}{3}$ pound walnuts cost $1.75, does she have enough money?

_____   _____

Problem-Solving Strategy

Draw a Diagram

Draw a diagram to solve.

1. Three students want to compare the heights of the plants they are growing in class. Bill's plant is $\frac{11}{12}$ feet tall, Karen's is $\frac{3}{4}$ feet tall, and Lois' is $\frac{5}{6}$ feet tall. List the heights from least to greatest.

_____

2. Charlie cut a cake into 18 pieces. He decorated $\frac{2}{9}$ of the pieces blue, $\frac{1}{3}$ yellow, $\frac{2}{6}$ green, and $\frac{1}{9}$ red. How many pieces of each color are there?

_____

_____

3. Peter shared a bag of 16 pencils with his friends. He gave $\frac{1}{4}$ to Mark, $\frac{3}{8}$ to Sue, and the rest to Pat. How many pencils did Pat get?

_____

4. Nancy needs $\frac{2}{3}$ yard blue ribbon, $\frac{3}{8}$ yard white fabric, $\frac{7}{8}$ yard red felt, and $\frac{3}{4}$ yard wood for a project. List her supplies from greatest to least.

_____

Mixed Applications

Solve:

_____

CHOOSE A STRATEGY

- **Make an Organized List**   • **Work Backward**   • **Write a Number Sentence**   • **Find a Pattern**

5. Jeff has 4 cookies left after sharing with his friends. He gave 3 to Pete, 6 to Sam, 4 to Brett, and 2 to Sally. How many cookies did he originally have?

_____

6. On Monday Susan walked 1 mile. On Tuesday she walked 1.5 miles; on Wednesday, 2.5 miles; and on Thursday, 4 miles. If the pattern continues, how far will she walk on Friday?

_____

7. Mr. Wong asked the 36 students in his class what type of book they liked to read. The table at the right shows their responses. What is the most popular type of book? the least popular?

_____

Popular Book Types	
Mysteries	$\frac{2}{4}$
Biographies	$\frac{1}{18}$
Science fiction	$\frac{4}{9}$

Name _____

Prime and Composite Numbers

Vocabulary

Fill in the blanks.

1. _____ have exactly two factors,
   1 and the number itself.

2. _____ have more than two factors.

Use the grid below to draw all the rectangles that can be made
using each number. Each square equals one unit. Record the length
and the width of each rectangle.

3. 8 _____   4. 7 _____   5. 12 _____

_____   _____   _____

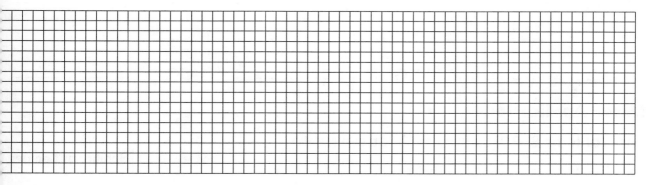

Write *prime* or *composite* for each number.

6. 11 _____   7. 16 _____   8. 37 _____

Mixed Applications

9. The area of Sharon's garden
   is 40 sq ft. List all the possible
   lengths and widths of Sharon's
   garden.

10. Beth has $0.60 more than Suzy.
    Together they have $8.20. How
    much money does each girl
    have?

_____   _____

_____   _____

Factors and Greatest Common Factors

Vocabulary

Fill in the blanks.

1. The greatest factor that two or more numbers have in common

   is the _____, or _____.

List the factors of each number.

2. 6

3. 20

4. 32

_____   _____   _____

List the factors of each number. Write the greatest common factor
for each pair of numbers.

5.   6 _____   6.   9 _____   7.   15 _____

      8 _____   12 _____   21 _____

   GCF _____   GCF _____   GCF _____

Mixed Applications

For Problems 8–10, use the table at the right.

8. The tennis team is selling packs
   of homemade cookies as a fund
   raiser. They want to pack the
   cookies in bags that hold the same
   number of one kind of cookie.
   What is the greatest number of
   cookies they can pack in each bag?

Cookie	Number of Cookies
Chocolate chip	24
Oatmeal	36
Raisin	16
Butterscotch	12
Lemon	28

_____

9. The tennis team buys empty
   bags in packages of 10. How
   many bags in all are needed to
   pack the cookies? How many
   packages of bags are needed?

10. The tennis team sells cookies for
    $0.75 per bag. If they sell 22 bags
    of cookies, how much money will
    the tennis team make?

_____   _____

Name _____

Equivalent Fractions

Vocabulary

Fill in the blank.

1. Fractions that name the same amount are called _____.

_____

Use the number lines to name an equivalent
fraction for each.

2. $\dfrac{1}{4}$ _____   **3.** $\dfrac{4}{8}$ _____   **4.** $\dfrac{3}{4}$ _____

Find an equivalent fraction. Use multiplication or division.

5. $\dfrac{2}{4}$ _____   **6.** $\dfrac{18}{20}$ _____   **7.** $\dfrac{3}{8}$ _____   **8.** $\dfrac{7}{21}$ _____

9. $\dfrac{3}{5}$ _____   **10.** $\dfrac{2}{15}$ _____   **11.** $\dfrac{8}{12}$ _____   **12.** $\dfrac{10}{16}$ _____

Which fraction is *not* equivalent to the given fraction? Circle *a*, *b*, or *c*.

13. $\dfrac{2}{3}$ **a.** $\dfrac{6}{9}$ **b.** $\dfrac{5}{6}$ **c.** $\dfrac{8}{12}$ **14.** $\dfrac{9}{15}$ **a.** $\dfrac{3}{5}$ **b.** $\dfrac{18}{30}$ **c.** $\dfrac{16}{25}$

15. $\dfrac{6}{8}$ **a.** $\dfrac{10}{12}$ **b.** $\dfrac{3}{4}$ **c.** $\dfrac{24}{32}$ **16.** $\dfrac{3}{7}$ **a.** $\dfrac{6}{14}$ **b.** $\dfrac{14}{28}$ **c.** $\dfrac{21}{49}$

Mixed Applications

17. René and 6 friends decide to
order lasagna. Each tray of
lasagna is cut into 12 pieces.
How many trays of lasagna will
they have to buy in order for
everyone to get 3 pieces? How
many pieces will be left over?

_____

_____

18. Andy bought a pack of 16 pencils
and gave 4 pencils away to
friends. Write two equivalent
fractions to represent the part of
the pencils that Andy gave away.

_____

_____

Problem-Solving Strategy

Draw a Diagram

Draw a diagram to solve.

1. At a baseball game, Ben spent $\frac{4}{12}$ of his money on tickets and $\frac{1}{4}$ of his money on food. On which item did Ben spend more money? Explain how you know.

_____

_____

2. Juliana bought 21 drinks, 14 of which are fruit punch. Toby said that $\frac{2}{3}$ of the drinks are fruit punch. Is Toby right? Explain.

_____

3. Alan bought a package containing 16 peaches. He gave 4 peaches to his uncle and 8 to his mother. Write two equivalent fractions to describe the fraction of the package of peaches that is left.

_____

Mixed Applications

Solve.

CHOOSE A STRATEGY

• **Draw a Diagram**   • **Find a Pattern**   • **Make a Model**   • **Guess and Check**   • **Work Backward**

4. Julie spent half her money on lunch. Then she spent half her remaining money on a magazine. She has $4.50 left. How much money did Julie begin with?

_____

_____

5. The length of Alice's rectangular garden is twice its width. The perimeter of the garden is 48 feet. What are the length and width of the garden?

_____

_____

Simplest Form

Is the fraction in its simplest form? Write *yes* or *no*.

1. $\dfrac{3}{4}$ _____

2. $\dfrac{6}{8}$ _____

3. $\dfrac{7}{21}$ _____

4. $\dfrac{14}{15}$ _____

5. $\dfrac{12}{15}$ _____

6. $\dfrac{7}{9}$ _____

Write each fraction in its simplest form.

7. $\dfrac{4}{10}$ _____

8. $\dfrac{3}{8}$ _____

9. $\dfrac{6}{12}$ _____

10. $\dfrac{6}{15}$ _____

11. $\dfrac{2}{3}$ _____

12. $\dfrac{4}{16}$ _____

13. $\dfrac{2}{8}$ _____

14. $\dfrac{8}{12}$ _____

15. $\dfrac{8}{24}$ _____

16. $\dfrac{3}{9}$ _____

17. $\dfrac{4}{15}$ _____

18. $\dfrac{7}{17}$ _____

Mixed Applications

19. Four students stand in line. Ken is after Jim and before Gary. Andy is after Jim and before Ken. If Ken is next to Gary, in what order are the students?

_____

20. Gil bought 6 CDs on Friday. He now has 48 CDs. What fraction of his CDs did he buy on Friday? Write your answer in the simplest form.

_____

21. Jean-Paul uses $\frac{1}{3}$ cup walnuts, $\frac{1}{8}$ cup chocolate chips, and $\frac{1}{2}$ cup coconut in his cookie recipe. Of these ingredients, which is used the most? Use fraction bars to explain your answer.

_____

_____

22. Mary ran $\frac{3}{4}$ mile, Lila ran $\frac{2}{3}$ mile, and Sue ran $\frac{3}{8}$ mile. Who ran the farthest? Draw a diagram to solve.

_____

_____

More About Simplest Form

Vocabulary

Fill in the blank.

1. A fraction is in _____ when the greatest common factor, or GCF, of the numerator and denominator is 1.

Is the fraction in simplest form? Write *yes* or *no*. If it is not in simplest form, write it in simplest form.

2. $\frac{6}{8}$ _____

3. $\frac{2}{3}$ _____

4. $\frac{3}{6}$ _____

5. $\frac{7}{10}$ _____

6. $\frac{5}{30}$ _____

7. $\frac{3}{24}$ _____

Write each fraction in simplest form.

8. $\frac{15}{30}$ _____

9. $\frac{4}{9}$ _____

10. $\frac{5}{40}$ _____

11. $\frac{7}{21}$ _____

12. $\frac{10}{24}$ _____

13. $\frac{20}{22}$ _____

14. $\frac{3}{18}$ _____

15. $\frac{24}{42}$ _____

16. $\frac{9}{36}$ _____

Mixed Applications

17. Dexter brought in 7 cans of food for the local food bank. His class brought in 35 cans in all. Write in the simplest form the fraction of cans Dexter brought in.

_____

18. Rita received $60 for her birthday and put $36 in her savings account. Write in the simplest form the fraction of her present that Rita saved.

_____

19. It takes Gloria 8 minutes to bake a batch of cookies. How long will it take her to bake 14 batches?

_____

20. Shana has 6 white rabbits. She has 3 times as many brown rabbits. How many brown rabbits does she have? How many in all?

_____

Adding Like Fractions

Write an addition sentence for each drawing.

1.

1

$\frac{1}{8}$	$\frac{1}{8}$	$\frac{1}{8}$	$\frac{1}{8}$	$\frac{1}{8}$

_____

2.

1

$\frac{1}{4}$	$\frac{1}{4}$

_____

3.

1

$\frac{1}{5}$	$\frac{1}{5}$	$\frac{1}{5}$	$\frac{1}{5}$

_____

4.

1

$\frac{1}{10}$	$\frac{1}{10}$	$\frac{1}{10}$	$\frac{1}{10}$	$\frac{1}{10}$	$\frac{1}{10}$	$\frac{1}{10}$	$\frac{1}{10}$	$\frac{1}{10}$	$\frac{1}{10}$

_____

5.

1	1

$\frac{1}{6}$	$\frac{1}{6}$	$\frac{1}{6}$	$\frac{1}{6}$	$\frac{1}{6}$	$\frac{1}{6}$	$\frac{1}{6}$

_____

Use fraction strips to find the sum. Write the answer in simplest form.

6. $\frac{2}{7} + \frac{4}{7}$

_____

7. $\frac{1}{6} + \frac{1}{6}$

_____

8. $\frac{4}{10} + \frac{7}{10}$

_____

9. $\frac{2}{3} + \frac{1}{3}$

_____

10. $\frac{3}{4} + \frac{3}{4}$

_____

11. $\frac{7}{8} + \frac{3}{8}$

_____

Mixed Applications

12. Jack bought a box of pencils. He gave $\frac{2}{7}$ to Max and $\frac{1}{7}$ to Jean. How much of the box of pencils did he give away?

_____

13. Janet wants to buy 3 CDs that cost $17.99 each. How much will they cost in all?

_____

Adding Unlike Fractions

Use fraction bars to find the sum.

1.

1

$\frac{1}{3}$	$\frac{1}{3}$	$\frac{1}{6}$

_____

2.

1

$\frac{1}{4}$	$\frac{1}{4}$	$\frac{1}{8}$	$\frac{1}{8}$	$\frac{1}{8}$

_____

3.

1

$\frac{1}{3}$	$\frac{1}{3}$	$\frac{1}{4}$

_____

4.

1

$\frac{1}{2}$	$\frac{1}{5}$

_____

5.

1

$\frac{1}{12}$	$\frac{1}{12}$	$\frac{1}{12}$	$\frac{1}{3}$

_____

6.

1

$\frac{1}{10}$	$\frac{1}{10}$	$\frac{1}{10}$	$\frac{1}{5}$

_____

Use fraction bars to find the sum.

7. $\frac{1}{3} + \frac{1}{6}$

_____

8. $\frac{5}{8} + \frac{3}{4}$

_____

9. $\frac{3}{4} + \frac{1}{6}$

_____

10. $\frac{7}{10} + \frac{2}{5}$

_____

11. $\frac{4}{10} + \frac{3}{5}$

_____

12. $\frac{4}{5} + \frac{7}{10}$

_____

Mixed Applications

13. Lewis ran $\frac{2}{3}$ of a mile on Monday and $\frac{5}{12}$ of a mile on Tuesday. How many miles did he run in all?

_____

14. Alicia went to the fair with $20.00. She bought 2 drinks for $2.25 each and 1 pretzel for $1.89. T-shirts cost $5.99 each. How many T-shirts can she buy?

_____

Using the Least Common Denominator to Add Fractions

Vocabulary

Complete.

1. The least common multiple, or LCM, of two or more denominators

is called the _____.

Use the LCM to name the least common denominator, or LCD, for each pair of fractions.

2. $\frac{1}{3}$ and $\frac{1}{6}$

_____

3. $\frac{1}{12}$ and $\frac{1}{4}$

_____

4. $\frac{1}{10}$ and $\frac{1}{2}$

_____

5. $\frac{1}{9}$ and $\frac{1}{3}$

_____

6. $\frac{1}{2}$ and $\frac{1}{5}$

_____

7. $\frac{1}{8}$ and $\frac{1}{2}$

_____

8. $\frac{1}{3}$ and $\frac{1}{12}$

_____

9. $\frac{1}{2}$ and $\frac{1}{4}$

_____

Use fraction strips to find the sum. Write the answer in simplest form.

10. $\frac{3}{5} + \frac{3}{10}$

_____

11. $\frac{5}{6} + \frac{7}{12}$

_____

12. $\frac{2}{3} + \frac{1}{9}$

_____

13. $\frac{1}{2} + \frac{4}{5}$

_____

14. $\frac{1}{6} + \frac{2}{3}$

_____

15. $\frac{9}{12} + \frac{1}{3}$

_____

16. $\frac{3}{4} + \frac{5}{8}$

_____

17. $\frac{2}{6} + \frac{2}{3}$

_____

Mixed Applications

18. Clara's family has 12 pets. There are 3 rabbits, 4 cats, and 5 dogs. What fraction of the pets are cats?

_____

19. Roberto bought $\frac{1}{9}$ of a set of trading cards last week. He bought $\frac{2}{3}$ of the set this week. What fraction of a set does Roberto have in all?

_____

Adding Three Fractions

Use the LCM to name the least common denominator, or LCD, for
each group of fractions.

1. $\frac{1}{3}, \frac{1}{4},$ and $\frac{1}{2}$

2. $\frac{1}{4}, \frac{1}{6},$ and $\frac{1}{12}$

3. $\frac{1}{10}, \frac{1}{2},$ and $\frac{1}{5}$

_____

_____

_____

4. $\frac{1}{2}, \frac{1}{6},$ and $\frac{1}{3}$

5. $\frac{1}{6}, \frac{1}{3},$ and $\frac{1}{4}$

6. $\frac{1}{12}, \frac{1}{6},$ and $\frac{1}{4}$

_____

_____

_____

Use the fraction strips to find the sum. Write the answer in
simplest form.

7. $\frac{2}{3} + \frac{1}{6} + \frac{2}{6}$

8. $\frac{3}{5} + \frac{7}{10} + \frac{1}{2}$

9. $\frac{1}{9} + \frac{2}{3} + \frac{5}{9}$

_____

_____

_____

10. $\frac{1}{12} + \frac{2}{3} + \frac{1}{4}$

11. $\frac{1}{3} + \frac{1}{4} + \frac{2}{6}$

12. $\frac{1}{3} + \frac{3}{4} + \frac{1}{6}$

_____

_____

_____

13. $\frac{5}{8} + \frac{1}{2} + \frac{7}{8}$

14. $\frac{4}{6} + \frac{1}{6} + \frac{3}{12}$

15. $\frac{2}{4} + \frac{7}{8} + \frac{1}{4}$

_____

_____

_____

16. $\frac{3}{4} + \frac{2}{3} + \frac{1}{6}$

17. $\frac{1}{2} + \frac{1}{4} + \frac{3}{6}$

18. $\frac{1}{10} + \frac{1}{5} + \frac{1}{2}$

_____

_____

_____

Mixed Applications

19. An auditorium has 3 sections of
seats. Each section has 15 rows
with 12 seats in each row. How
many people can be seated in
the auditorium?

20. Pete sees two equal-size punch
bowls. One bowl is $\frac{3}{10}$ full, and
the other is $\frac{2}{5}$ full. If he pours the
punch from one bowl into the
other, how full is the bowl with
the combined punch?

_____

_____

Problem-Solving Strategy

Make a Model

Make a model to solve.

1. Samantha bought 3 packets of stickers. Each packet contains 100 stickers. If she divides all of the stickers evenly among 6 friends and herself, how many stickers are left over?

2. One day, $\frac{1}{8}$ of the patients brought to a veterinary hospital were rabbits, $\frac{1}{2}$ were cats, and $\frac{1}{4}$ were dogs. What part of all the patients were rabbits, cats, and dogs that day?

3. James uses $\frac{5}{6}$ meter of butcher paper to make one sign. How many meters of paper will he need to make 3 signs?

4. Brent decorated $\frac{3}{8}$ of his sugar cookies with blue frosting, $\frac{1}{4}$ with yellow frosting, and $\frac{3}{8}$ with purple frosting. What part of the cookies were frosted?

Mixed Applications

Solve.

$\overbrace{\qquad\qquad}^{\text{CHOOSE A STRATEGY}}$

- **Make an Organized List** • **Work Backward** • **Act It Out** • **Use a Table** • **Make a Model**

5. During the week, Carrie spent $3.50 for a book. The next day her father gave her $1.25. Then she went to a movie, which cost $7.50. If she now has $10.25, how much money did she have at the beginning of the week?

6. A pizza parlor has a special offer of a minipizza with one topping. Customers can choose thin or thick crust, and they have 4 choices of toppings: pepperoni, sausage, extra cheese, or olives. How many choices do customers have?

Subtracting Like Fractions

Use fraction strips to find the difference.

1. $\dfrac{5}{6} - \dfrac{4}{6} = n$ _____

2. $\dfrac{6}{12} - \dfrac{1}{12} = n$ _____

3. $\dfrac{4}{5} - \dfrac{2}{5} = n$ _____

$\frac{1}{6}$	$\frac{1}{6}$	$\frac{1}{6}$	$\frac{1}{6}$	$\frac{1}{6}$

$\frac{1}{12}$	$\frac{1}{12}$	$\frac{1}{12}$	$\frac{1}{12}$	$\frac{1}{12}$	$\frac{1}{12}$

$\frac{1}{5}$	$\frac{1}{5}$	$\frac{1}{5}$	$\frac{1}{5}$

4. $\dfrac{7}{8} - \dfrac{2}{8} = n$ _____

5. $\dfrac{7}{9} - \dfrac{2}{9} = n$ _____

6. $\dfrac{8}{10} - \dfrac{5}{10} = n$ _____

$\frac{1}{8}$	$\frac{1}{8}$	$\frac{1}{8}$	$\frac{1}{8}$	$\frac{1}{8}$	$\frac{1}{8}$	$\frac{1}{8}$

$\frac{1}{9}$	$\frac{1}{9}$	$\frac{1}{9}$	$\frac{1}{9}$	$\frac{1}{9}$	$\frac{1}{9}$	$\frac{1}{9}$

$\frac{1}{10}$	$\frac{1}{10}$	$\frac{1}{10}$	$\frac{1}{10}$	$\frac{1}{10}$	$\frac{1}{10}$	$\frac{1}{10}$	$\frac{1}{10}$

Use fraction strips to find the difference. Write the answer in simplest form.

7. $\dfrac{6}{8} - \dfrac{4}{8} = n$ _____

8. $\dfrac{5}{6} - \dfrac{2}{6} = n$ _____

9. $\dfrac{9}{10} - \dfrac{4}{10} = n$ _____

$\frac{1}{8}$	$\frac{1}{8}$	$\frac{1}{8}$	$\frac{1}{8}$	$\frac{1}{8}$	$\frac{1}{8}$

$\frac{1}{6}$	$\frac{1}{6}$	$\frac{1}{6}$	$\frac{1}{6}$	$\frac{1}{6}$

$\frac{1}{10}$	$\frac{1}{10}$	$\frac{1}{10}$	$\frac{1}{10}$	$\frac{1}{10}$	$\frac{1}{10}$	$\frac{1}{10}$	$\frac{1}{10}$	$\frac{1}{10}$

10. $\dfrac{11}{12} - \dfrac{7}{12} = n$ _____

11. $\dfrac{2}{4} - \dfrac{1}{4} = n$ _____

12. $\dfrac{8}{9} - \dfrac{5}{9} = n$ _____

$\frac{1}{12}$	$\frac{1}{12}$	$\frac{1}{12}$	$\frac{1}{12}$	$\frac{1}{12}$	$\frac{1}{12}$	$\frac{1}{12}$	$\frac{1}{12}$	$\frac{1}{12}$	$\frac{1}{12}$	$\frac{1}{12}$

$\frac{1}{4}$	$\frac{1}{4}$

$\frac{1}{9}$	$\frac{1}{9}$	$\frac{1}{9}$	$\frac{1}{9}$	$\frac{1}{9}$	$\frac{1}{9}$	$\frac{1}{9}$	$\frac{1}{9}$

Mixed Applications

13. Phil biked $\dfrac{2}{8}$ mile on Monday and $\dfrac{5}{8}$ mile on Tuesday. On which day did he bike farther? How much farther did he bike?

14. When Terry arrived at the party, $\dfrac{9}{12}$ of the cake was left. She ate $\dfrac{2}{12}$ of the cake. How much was left after Terry ate?

_____

_____

Subtracting Unlike Fractions

Use fraction bars to find the difference.

1.
$\frac{1}{2}$	
$\frac{1}{12}$ $\frac{1}{12}$ $\frac{1}{12}$	?

_____

2.
$\frac{1}{3}$	
$\frac{1}{9}$ $\frac{1}{9}$	?

_____

3.
$\frac{1}{4}$	$\frac{1}{4}$	$\frac{1}{4}$
$\frac{1}{8}$ $\frac{1}{8}$	?	

_____

4.
$\frac{1}{3}$	$\frac{1}{3}$
$\frac{1}{12}$ $\frac{1}{12}$ $\frac{1}{12}$ $\frac{1}{12}$ $\frac{1}{12}$	?

_____

5.
$\frac{1}{10}$ $\frac{1}{10}$ $\frac{1}{10}$ $\frac{1}{10}$ $\frac{1}{10}$ $\frac{1}{10}$ $\frac{1}{10}$
$\frac{1}{5}$ $\frac{1}{5}$ $\frac{1}{5}$?

_____

6.
$\frac{1}{12}$ $\frac{1}{12}$ $\frac{1}{12}$ $\frac{1}{12}$ $\frac{1}{12}$ $\frac{1}{12}$ $\frac{1}{12}$ $\frac{1}{12}$ $\frac{1}{12}$ $\frac{1}{12}$ $\frac{1}{12}$
$\frac{1}{4}$ $\frac{1}{4}$ $\frac{1}{4}$?

_____

7. $\dfrac{4}{5} - \dfrac{3}{10} = n$

_____

8. $\dfrac{4}{6} - \dfrac{5}{12} = n$

_____

9. $\dfrac{5}{6} - \dfrac{5}{12} = n$

_____

10. $\dfrac{1}{2} - \dfrac{4}{10} = n$

_____

11. $\dfrac{6}{8} - \dfrac{1}{2} = n$

_____

12. $\dfrac{2}{3} - \dfrac{3}{6} = n$

_____

13. $\dfrac{1}{2} - \dfrac{1}{8} = n$

_____

14. $\dfrac{9}{12} - \dfrac{2}{3} = n$

_____

15. $\dfrac{4}{6} - \dfrac{1}{12} = n$

_____

16. $\dfrac{7}{8} - \dfrac{1}{4} = n$

_____

17. $\dfrac{11}{12} - \dfrac{1}{3} = n$

_____

18. $\dfrac{4}{6} - \dfrac{1}{2} = n$

_____

Mixed Applications

19. Joyce went to Camp Mattatuch for $\frac{3}{4}$ of a month. She spent $\frac{2}{8}$ of the time swimming, $\frac{1}{4}$ of the time doing crafts, and the rest hiking. What fraction of the month did she hike?

_____

20. On a recent bicycle trip, Karen rode 75 miles in 6 days. If she rode the same number of miles each day, how many miles per day did she ride?

_____

Using the Least Common Denominator to Subtract Fractions

Name the least common denominator, or LCD, for each pair of fractions.

1. $\frac{1}{5}$ and $\frac{1}{10}$

2. $\frac{1}{3}$ and $\frac{1}{6}$

3. $\frac{1}{6}$ and $\frac{1}{4}$

_____ _____ _____

4. $\frac{1}{2}$ and $\frac{1}{8}$

5. $\frac{1}{2}$ and $\frac{1}{6}$

6. $\frac{1}{5}$ and $\frac{1}{4}$

_____ _____ _____

Use fraction strips to find the difference. Write the answer in simplest form.

7. $\frac{5}{8} - \frac{1}{2} =$ _____

8. $\frac{2}{3} - \frac{5}{9} =$ _____

9. $\frac{5}{6} - \frac{1}{3} =$ _____

10. $\frac{9}{12} - \frac{2}{3} =$ _____

11. $\frac{5}{8} - \frac{1}{4} =$ _____

12. $\frac{4}{5} - \frac{1}{10} =$ _____

13. $\frac{5}{12} - \frac{1}{4} =$ _____

14. $\frac{4}{5} - \frac{2}{10} =$ _____

15. $\frac{4}{6} - \frac{1}{3} =$ _____

Mixed Applications

16. Tony spent $\frac{3}{4}$ of the afternoon studying for the math test. Julie spent $\frac{2}{3}$ of the afternoon studying for the test. How much longer did Tony spend studying than Judy?

_____

17. Victoria was saving for a bike. She earned $\frac{3}{5}$ of the money working for her neighbors and $\frac{3}{10}$ working for her parents. The rest she got for her birthday. What fraction of the money did she get for her birthday?

_____

18. Mr. Rafael bought 525 stars for his class. He wants to give each of his 35 students an equal number of stars. How many stars should each student get?

_____

19. Joe drank $\frac{5}{8}$ of a glass of milk. Later in the day, he drank another $\frac{3}{4}$ glass of milk. How many glasses of milk did he drink?

_____

Subtracting Fractions Using a Ruler

Use the ruler to find the difference.

1. $\dfrac{13}{16}$ in. $-$ $\dfrac{4}{16}$ in. $= n$

2. $\dfrac{5}{8}$ in. $-$ $\dfrac{2}{8}$ in. $= n$

3. 1 in. $-$ $\dfrac{3}{4}$ in. $= n$

_____

_____

_____

4. $\dfrac{3}{8}$ in. $-$ $\dfrac{1}{4}$ in. $= n$

5. $\dfrac{13}{16}$ in. $-$ $\dfrac{5}{8}$ in. $= n$

6. $\dfrac{7}{8}$ in. $-$ $\dfrac{3}{4}$ in. $= n$

_____

_____

_____

7. $\dfrac{9}{16}$ in. $-$ $\dfrac{3}{8}$ in. $= n$

8. 1 in. $-$ $\dfrac{5}{8}$ in. $= n$

9. $\dfrac{1}{2}$ in. $-$ $\dfrac{1}{4}$ in. $= n$

_____

_____

_____

Mixed Applications

For Problems 10–11, use a ruler to solve.

10. Henry collects miniature animals. His longest animal is $\dfrac{15}{16}$ inch long. His shortest animal is $\dfrac{3}{8}$ inch long. What is the difference in length between the two animals?

_____

11. Jake jumped $\dfrac{7}{8}$ inch farther than Ted. Phil jumped $\dfrac{3}{4}$ inch farther than Ted. How much farther did Jake jump than Phil?

_____

Problem-Solving Strategy

Work Backward

Work backward to solve.

1. Jerry's kitten is 19 cm tall and is 6 months old. The kitten grew 2 cm between the ages of 5 months and 6 months. It grew 3 cm between the ages of 4 months and 5 months. How tall was Jerry's kitten when it was 4 months old?

_____

2. Denise went shopping at the mall. She spent $11.35 on a new T-shirt and $2.25 for hair ribbons. Lunch cost $4.50, and a drink cost $1.25. She came home with $10.65. How much money did Denise have before she went to the mall?

_____

3. Kirk grew a crystal in science class. On Monday it was $\frac{13}{16}$ inch tall. It had grown $\frac{1}{4}$ inch between Friday and Monday. It had grown $\frac{1}{2}$ inch between Tuesday and Friday. How tall was Kirk's crystal on Tuesday?

_____

4. Terry planted a gladiolus bulb. On Wednesday it was $\frac{7}{8}$ inch tall. It had grown $\frac{1}{4}$ inch between Tuesday and Wednesday. It had grown $\frac{3}{8}$ inch between Monday and Tuesday. How tall was Terry's gladiolus on Monday?

_____

Mixed Applications

Solve.

CHOOSE A STRATEGY

• **Work Backward** • **Write a Number Sentence** • **Guess and Check** • **Make an Organized List**

5. Morgan's class reads every day in class. On Mondays, Wednesdays, and Fridays they read for 1 hour each day. On Tuesdays and Thursdays they read for $\frac{1}{2}$ hour each day. How many hours do they read each week?

_____

6. Lisa gave 10 sheets of graph paper to Ted and 8 sheets to Nancy. Then Jill gave Lisa 12 sheets of graph paper. Lisa now has 35 sheets. How many sheets did she have to begin with?

_____

Name _____

Estimating Sums and Differences

Use the number lines to estimate whether the fraction is closest to 0, to $\frac{1}{2}$, or to 1.

1. $\frac{4}{10}$

2. $\frac{11}{12}$

3. $\frac{2}{10}$

4. $\frac{7}{12}$

_____   _____   _____   _____

Write whether the fraction is closest to 0, to $\frac{1}{2}$, or to 1. You may use a number line.

5. $\frac{7}{8}$

6. $\frac{3}{8}$

7. $\frac{2}{9}$

8. $\frac{1}{8}$

_____   _____   _____   _____

Estimate each sum or difference.

9. $\frac{1}{2} + \frac{3}{4}$

10. $\frac{1}{2} + \frac{5}{8}$

11. $\frac{1}{4} + \frac{5}{9}$

12. $\frac{6}{8} + \frac{2}{4}$

_____   _____   _____   _____

13. $\frac{11}{12} - \frac{1}{9}$

14. $\frac{5}{6} - \frac{3}{5}$

15. $\frac{8}{9} - \frac{3}{4}$

16. $\frac{7}{9} - \frac{5}{8}$

_____   _____   _____   _____

Mixed Applications

17. Joanna talked on the phone for $\frac{3}{5}$ hour before dinner. She talked on the phone for $\frac{7}{8}$ hour after dinner. About how long did she talk in all?

18. Yolanda runs 3 miles a day, and Rob runs 2 miles a day. They run every day in March. How many miles do they run in all during March?

_____   _____

Adding and Subtracting Like Fractions

Find the sum. Write the answer in simplest form.

1. $\frac{5}{7} + \frac{1}{7} = n$

2. $\frac{4}{9} + \frac{3}{9} = n$

3. $\frac{4}{12} + \frac{8}{12} = n$

4. $\frac{3}{11} + \frac{7}{11} = n$

_____   _____   _____   _____

5. $\frac{2}{8} + \frac{4}{8} = n$

6. $\frac{7}{15} + \frac{4}{15} = n$

7. $\frac{5}{9} + \frac{1}{9} = n$

8. $\frac{1}{4} + \frac{2}{4} = n$

_____   _____   _____   _____

Find the difference. Write the answer in simplest form.

9. $\frac{4}{7} - \frac{2}{7} = n$

10. $\frac{3}{5} - \frac{1}{5} = n$

11. $\frac{6}{12} - \frac{2}{12} = n$

12. $\frac{3}{4} - \frac{2}{4} = n$

_____   _____   _____   _____

13. $\frac{7}{9} - \frac{2}{9} = n$

14. $\frac{4}{6} - \frac{1}{6} = n$

15. $\frac{3}{8} - \frac{2}{8} = n$

16. $\frac{9}{10} - \frac{5}{10} = n$

_____   _____   _____   _____

Mixed Applications

17. George ran $\frac{3}{8}$ mile on Sunday and $\frac{2}{8}$ mile on Monday. How much farther did George run on Sunday than on Monday?

18. Lona pulled the wagon for $\frac{4}{10}$ hour. Eric pulled the wagon for $\frac{1}{10}$ hour. For how long did they pull the wagon in all?

_____   _____

19. Mary and her friends went to the amusement park. They left home at 8:30 A.M. They drove 1 hour 15 minutes to the park. They spent 6 hours at the park. Then they drove 1 hour 15 minutes home. What time was it when they returned home?

20. Josh had a great time at the amusement park with Mary and all their friends. Josh spent $10.75 on souvenirs, $4.50 on lunch, and $3.00 on gas. How much money did he have left from his $20 bill?

_____   _____

Adding and Subtracting Unlike Fractions

Find the sum or difference. Write the answer in simplest form.

1. $\frac{1}{2} + \frac{2}{8} = n$

2. $\frac{2}{5} + \frac{1}{3} = n$

3. $\frac{6}{8} + \frac{1}{4} = n$

4. $\frac{9}{12} - \frac{2}{4} = n$

_____ _____ _____ _____

5. $\frac{8}{16} - \frac{2}{8} = n$

6. $\frac{2}{10} + \frac{3}{5} = n$

7. $\frac{7}{9} - \frac{1}{3} = n$

8. $\frac{4}{15} + \frac{2}{3} = n$

_____ _____ _____ _____

9. $\frac{3}{8} - \frac{1}{4} = n$

10. $\frac{6}{12} - \frac{2}{6} = n$

11. $\frac{9}{10} - \frac{4}{5} = n$

12. $\frac{6}{8} - \frac{1}{2} = n$

_____ _____ _____ _____

13. $\frac{5}{8} + \frac{5}{16} = n$

14. $\frac{4}{5} + \frac{1}{10} = n$

15. $\frac{5}{9} - \frac{7}{18} = n$

16. $\frac{1}{2} - \frac{3}{14} = n$

_____ _____ _____ _____

17. $\frac{2}{20} + \frac{4}{5} = n$

18. $\frac{1}{3} - \frac{2}{9} = n$

19. $\frac{2}{6} - \frac{5}{18} = n$

20. $\frac{3}{8} + \frac{2}{4} = n$

_____ _____ _____ _____

Mixed Applications

21. Jade swam $\frac{1}{2}$ mile on Monday. On Wednesday she swam $\frac{3}{8}$ mile. How many miles did Jade swim in all?

22. Mike has 6 photo albums. Each photo album has 36 pictures in it. How many pictures does Mike have in all?

_____ _____

23. Monty spent $\frac{4}{5}$ hour mowing his lawn. Then he spent $\frac{2}{10}$ hour mowing his neighbor's lawn. How much longer did it take Monty to mow his lawn than his neighbor's lawn?

24. Laura bought 24 bananas. She gave 12 of them to her sister and 8 of them to her brother. What fraction of the bananas did Laura have left?

_____ _____

Practicing Addition and Subtraction

Find the sum or difference. Write each answer in simplest form.

1. $\dfrac{3}{6} - \dfrac{1}{6} = n$

2. $\dfrac{5}{8} + \dfrac{3}{16} = n$

3. $\dfrac{1}{4} - \dfrac{2}{12} = n$

4. $\dfrac{8}{14} - \dfrac{7}{14} = n$

_____   _____   _____   _____

5. $\dfrac{8}{9} - \dfrac{4}{9} = n$

6. $\dfrac{4}{15} + \dfrac{3}{5} = n$

7. $\dfrac{5}{8} - \dfrac{3}{16} = n$

8. $\dfrac{3}{7} - \dfrac{2}{14} = n$

_____   _____   _____   _____

9. $\dfrac{6}{20} + \dfrac{2}{10} = n$

10. $\dfrac{1}{9} + \dfrac{2}{3} = n$

11. $\dfrac{1}{7} - \dfrac{2}{35} = n$

12. $\dfrac{5}{7} + \dfrac{1}{7} = n$

_____   _____   _____   _____

13. $\dfrac{3}{8} + \dfrac{5}{16} = n$

14. $\dfrac{7}{12} - \dfrac{1}{12} = n$

15. $\dfrac{3}{5} + \dfrac{1}{4} = n$

16. $\dfrac{7}{10} - \dfrac{2}{5} = n$

_____   _____   _____   _____

Mixed Applications

17. Deena made $\frac{2}{5}$ pound of spaghetti. She made $\frac{3}{4}$ pound of meatballs. How much more meatballs did Deena make than spaghetti?

_____

18. Roy had a box of popcorn. He ate $\frac{2}{3}$ of the popcorn, and his friends ate $\frac{2}{9}$ of the popcorn. What fraction of the box of popcorn is gone?

_____

19. Harry, Jane, and Richard went to the mall. They started with $64.00. When they finished, they had $23.75 left. How much money did they spend at the mall?

_____

20. Ed made 36 cookies on Monday. On Tuesday he made 29 cookies. He put 3 nuts on each cookie. How many nuts did Ed use on the cookies in all?

_____

Choosing Addition or Subtraction

Tell whether you would add or subtract to solve the problem. Solve.

1. Jenna practiced piano $\frac{1}{6}$ hour on Friday, $\frac{1}{2}$ hour on Saturday, and $\frac{2}{3}$ hour on Sunday. How long did Jenna practice in all?

   _____

2. Ellen ate $\frac{1}{8}$ of the pizza. Leslie ate $\frac{1}{4}$ of the pizza, and Allen ate $\frac{1}{2}$ of the pizza. What was the total amount of pizza eaten?

   _____

3. Matthew lives $\frac{3}{4}$ mile from school. Evan lives $\frac{3}{12}$ mile from school. How much farther does Matthew live from school than Evan?

   _____

4. Morgan spent $\frac{2}{3}$ of his money on models and $\frac{2}{9}$ of his money on school supplies. How much more of his money did he spend on models than on school supplies?

   _____

Mixed Applications

5. Alison gave $\frac{1}{6}$ of her hair ribbons to her sister. She gave $\frac{2}{3}$ of the ribbons to her friend. What fraction of the ribbons did Alison give away in all?

   _____

6. Colin spent $\frac{3}{8}$ of his paycheck on a backpack and $\frac{1}{2}$ of his paycheck on shoes. Did he spend more money for the backpack or for the shoes?

   _____

7. Al has 12 model airplanes. Steve has 3 times as many model airplanes as Al has. How many airplanes does Steve have? How many airplanes do they have in all?

   _____

8. Keesha lives $\frac{3}{10}$ mile from the soccer field. Sandy lives $\frac{4}{5}$ mile from the field. How much closer to the field does Keesha live than Sandy?

   _____

9. Mr. Reed is taking the 24 students in his class on a field trip. Each student has to pay $7 to go. How much money is Mr. Reed's class paying to go on the field trip?

   _____

10. Jim saw 10 blue jays, 12 robins, and 4 crows in his backyard. What fraction of the birds he saw were robins?

    _____

Problem-Solving Strategy

Draw a Diagram

Draw a diagram to solve.

1. Some Upper Crest Middle School students are taking a field trip. Of the students going, $\frac{1}{2}$ are sixth graders, $\frac{1}{4}$ are seventh graders, and $\frac{1}{4}$ are eighth graders. There are 20 seventh graders going. How many students are going on the field trip?

2. Brett rides his bike a set number of miles every week. On Sunday he rides $\frac{2}{5}$ of his total distance. On Tuesday he rides $\frac{1}{2}$ of the distance, and on Thursday he rides $\frac{1}{10}$ of the distance. He rides 7 miles on Thursday. How many miles does he ride for the week?

3. Doug collects mugs. In his mug collection, $\frac{1}{8}$ are clear, $\frac{1}{2}$ are black, and $\frac{3}{8}$ are multicolored. Doug has 6 clear mugs. How many mugs does Doug have in all?

4. Ralph, Melissa, and Peter are comparing their ages. At 36 years old, Ralph is 8 years older than Peter. Peter is 6 years younger than Melissa. How old is Melissa?

Mixed Applications

Solve.

CHOOSE A STRATEGY

• **Draw a Diagram**   • **Use a Table**   • **Write a Number Sentence**   • **Guess and Check**

5. Steve and Ellen bought 2 popcorns, 2 sodas, and 1 hot dog. How much did they spend in all?

Food	Price
Popcorn	$2.25
Soda	$1.00
Hot dog	$1.50

6. David has 50 mugs to take to the craft fair. If he carries them in boxes that hold 12 mugs, how many boxes will he take?

Name _____

Estimating Sums and Differences

Round the mixed number to the nearest $\frac{1}{2}$ or whole number. You
may use a number line or a ruler.

1. $2\frac{1}{4}$ **2.** $3\frac{1}{9}$ **3.** $4\frac{2}{3}$ **4.** $5\frac{7}{16}$ **5.** $7\frac{11}{12}$ **6.** $3\frac{5}{8}$

_____   _____   _____   _____   _____   _____

7. $6\frac{3}{4}$ **8.** $4\frac{7}{16}$ **9.** $8\frac{1}{3}$ **10.** $2\frac{7}{8}$ **11.** $7\frac{2}{8}$ **12.** $9\frac{4}{9}$

_____   _____   _____   _____   _____   _____

Estimate the sum or difference.

13. $3\frac{1}{4} + 2\frac{7}{8}$ **14.** $2\frac{1}{2} - 1\frac{3}{5}$ **15.** $5\frac{7}{12} + 3\frac{1}{8}$

_____   _____   _____

16. $7\frac{1}{9} - 1\frac{15}{16}$ **17.** $8\frac{2}{3} + 4\frac{3}{16}$ **18.** $6\frac{2}{9} + 4\frac{1}{12}$

_____   _____   _____

19. $8\frac{9}{10} - 5\frac{1}{5}$ **20.** $7\frac{14}{16} - 2\frac{8}{9}$ **21.** $9\frac{2}{8} + 3\frac{5}{12}$

_____   _____   _____

Mixed Applications

22. Mary earns $5.25 an hour baby-
sitting for her neighbors. Last
month she worked 87 hours. How
much money did she make?

_____

23. Franklin can type about 35 words
per minute. How long will it take
him to type 1,575 words?

_____

24. Sara buys $2\frac{5}{8}$ feet of cloth and
$3\frac{1}{4}$ feet of cloth. About how many
feet of cloth does she buy in all?

_____

25. Jack is making a project out of
wood. He started with a board
$3\frac{1}{2}$ feet long. He has used $2\frac{15}{16}$ feet
already. About how much does
he have left?

_____

Name _____

LESSON
20.2

Adding Mixed Numbers

Find the sum. You may wish to draw a picture.

1. $2\frac{3}{8}$
$+3\frac{1}{4}$

2. $4\frac{1}{3}$
$+3\frac{1}{6}$

3. $1\frac{5}{12}$
$+2\frac{1}{6}$

4. $3\frac{5}{8}$
$+3\frac{3}{4}$

5. $1\frac{1}{10}$
$+4\frac{2}{5}$

6. $3\frac{1}{9}$
$+4\frac{1}{3}$

7. $2\frac{3}{5}$
$+5\frac{7}{10}$

8. $4\frac{1}{12}$
$+2\frac{1}{3}$

9. $7\frac{2}{3} + 1\frac{5}{12} = n$ _____

10. $2\frac{4}{5} + 5\frac{3}{10} = n$ _____

11. $3\frac{1}{4} + 3\frac{7}{8} = n$ _____

12. $2\frac{2}{3} + 4\frac{1}{6} = n$ _____

13. $1\frac{1}{2} + 3\frac{5}{6} = n$ _____

14. $4\frac{2}{3} + 3\frac{5}{6} = n$ _____

15. $5\frac{5}{12} + 2\frac{1}{6} = n$ _____

16. $8\frac{2}{9} + 1\frac{1}{3} = n$ _____

Mixed Applications

17. Tim and Ralph are making a tower. They each built a separate section. Tim's section was $4\frac{7}{8}$ feet tall, and Ralph's section was $3\frac{1}{2}$ feet tall. How tall will the tower be when they join the sections?

18. At the last fifth-grade assembly, there were 5 classes with 31 students and 4 classes with 28 students. How many students attended the assembly?

19. Harriet and Felicia worked for the local charity on the weekend. Harriet worked $5\frac{1}{6}$ hours, and Felicia worked $3\frac{1}{4}$ hours. How many hours did the girls work together for the charity?

20. Jane's family traveled 171 miles on Monday and 377 miles on Tuesday. Philip's family traveled 396 miles on Monday and 211 miles on Tuesday. Whose family traveled more miles?

P116   ON MY OWN

Subtracting Mixed Numbers

Subtract. Write the answer in simplest form.

1. $3\frac{7}{10} = 3\frac{7}{10}$
   $-1\frac{2}{5} = 1\frac{4}{10}$

2. $5\frac{3}{4} = 5\frac{6}{8}$
   $-2\frac{1}{8} = 2\frac{1}{8}$

3. $8\frac{5}{6} = 8\frac{10}{12}$
   $-2\frac{1}{12} = 2\frac{1}{12}$

4. $7\frac{1}{2} = 7\frac{3}{6}$
   $-4\frac{1}{6} = 4\frac{1}{6}$

5. $9\frac{9}{10} = 9\frac{9}{10}$
   $-4\frac{3}{5} = 4\frac{6}{10}$

6. $5\frac{4}{9} = 5\frac{4}{9}$
   $-3\frac{1}{3} = 3\frac{3}{9}$

7. $7\frac{3}{8} - 2\frac{1}{4} = n$ _____

8. $5\frac{4}{5} - 3\frac{3}{10} = n$ _____

9. $3\frac{5}{12} - 2\frac{1}{4} = n$ _____

10. $5\frac{7}{12} - 3\frac{1}{2} = n$ _____

11. $9\frac{5}{6} - 4\frac{2}{3} = n$ _____

12. $4\frac{7}{8} - 2\frac{3}{4} = n$ _____

13. $6\frac{3}{4} - 4\frac{2}{8} = n$ _____

14. $3\frac{3}{4} - 2\frac{5}{8} = n$ _____

15. $4\frac{11}{12} - \frac{7}{12} = n$ _____

16. $5\frac{1}{2} - 3\frac{3}{8} = n$ _____

Mixed Applications

17. Sam made the chart at the right to keep track of how much wood he had for projects. He forgot to enter some of the numbers. Complete the table.

18. Each week Henry will work $3\frac{1}{2}$ hours on Wednesday and $4\frac{1}{4}$ hours on Friday. How many hours will he work each week?

_____

Type of Wood	Started With	Feet Used	Feet Left
Oak	$15\frac{1}{2}$	$9\frac{1}{4}$	_____
Pine	$22\frac{5}{8}$	_____	$10\frac{1}{4}$
Maple	_____	$12\frac{3}{4}$	$2\frac{1}{6}$
Cherry	$20\frac{3}{4}$	$5\frac{3}{8}$	_____

Problem-Solving Strategy

Work Backward

Work backward to solve.

1. Emily used wallpaper border to outline her window. She used $6\frac{1}{3}$ yards to outline the door and $1\frac{1}{6}$ yards to outline a shelf. She used $9\frac{1}{2}$ yards of border in all. How much border did she use on the window?

2. On Friday Jake had done a total of 125 push-ups in five days. He did 20 on Monday, 30 on Tuesday, 15 on Wednesday, and 20 on Thursday. How many push-ups did he do on Friday?

3. Dirk spent $3\frac{3}{4}$ hours outside on Saturday. During that time he spent $1\frac{1}{2}$ hours at the park and $1\frac{1}{4}$ hours in a friend's yard. He also rode his bicycle. How much time did he spend riding his bicycle?

4. Terry saved $60 to spend on a party for her mother. She spent $25 for a cake and $12 for party decorations. She spent the rest on a gift. How much did she spend on the gift?

Mixed Applications

Solve.

CHOOSE A STRATEGY

• **Work Backward**   • **Draw a Diagram**   • **Act it Out**   • **Write a Number Sentence**

5. Marlinda bought 32 inches of butcher paper for her project. She used $15\frac{1}{4}$ inches for the background and $12\frac{3}{4}$ inches for different parts of the project. How much butcher paper did she have left?

6. Ingrid planted a garden. In the garden $\frac{1}{2}$ of the rows are tomatoes, $\frac{1}{4}$ of the rows are green beans, and $\frac{2}{8}$ of the rows are lettuce. She has 5 rows of green beans. How many rows are in the garden?

Subtracting Mixed Numbers

Match the mixed number with the fraction bars.

1. $2\frac{1}{4}$ _____

2. $2\frac{3}{4}$ _____

3. $3\frac{3}{8}$ _____

a.

| 1 |

| $\frac{1}{4}$ | $\frac{1}{4}$ | $\frac{1}{4}$ | $\frac{1}{4}$ | $\frac{1}{4}$ | $\frac{1}{4}$ | $\frac{1}{4}$ |

b.

| 1 |

| 1 |

| $\frac{1}{8}$ | $\frac{1}{8}$ | $\frac{1}{8}$ | $\frac{1}{8}$ | $\frac{1}{8}$ | $\frac{1}{8}$ | $\frac{1}{8}$ | $\frac{1}{8}$ | $\frac{1}{8}$ |

c.

| 1 |

| $\frac{1}{4}$ | $\frac{1}{4}$ | $\frac{1}{4}$ | $\frac{1}{4}$ | $\frac{1}{4}$ |

Use fraction bars to find the difference.

4. $3\frac{2}{3}$
   $-\ \ \frac{1}{6}$
   _____

5. $7\frac{1}{4}$
   $-3\frac{3}{8}$
   _____

6. $4\frac{3}{10}$
   $-2\frac{4}{5}$
   _____

7. $6\frac{2}{3}$
   $-4\frac{5}{6}$
   _____

8. $8\frac{1}{2}$
   $-1\frac{5}{6}$
   _____

9. $3\frac{1}{8}$
   $-1\frac{1}{2}$
   _____

10. $7\frac{1}{10}$
    $-4\frac{2}{5}$
    _____

11. $10\frac{3}{8}$
    $-5\frac{3}{4}$
    _____

12. $6\frac{11}{12} - 2\frac{2}{3} = n$ _____

13. $4\frac{1}{5} - 1\frac{7}{10} = n$ _____

14. $5\frac{5}{8} - 1\frac{3}{4} = n$ _____

15. $5\frac{1}{2} - 2\frac{7}{12} = n$ _____

16. $8\frac{1}{6} - 4\frac{5}{12} = n$ _____

17. $7\frac{1}{4} - 6\frac{7}{12} = n$ _____

Mixed Applications

18. Stacey had $3\frac{3}{4}$ cakes for her party. She had $\frac{1}{8}$ of a cake left after the party. How much cake did Stacey use at her party?

_____

19. Martha spent $2\frac{1}{2}$ hours reading on Saturday. She spent $\frac{3}{4}$ of an hour reading on Sunday. How many hours did she spend reading this weekend?

_____

Precise Measurements

Vocabulary

Fill in the blank.

1. _____ means finding a unit that measures nearest to the actual length of an object.

For Problems 2–3, use a customary ruler.

2. Measure the length of the paper clip to the nearest $\frac{1}{8}$ inch.

3. Measure the length of the crayon to the nearest $\frac{1}{16}$ inch.

_____

_____

Draw a line to the given length.

4. $1\frac{3}{4}$ inch

5. $2\frac{3}{16}$ inch

6. $3\frac{5}{16}$ inch

Use a ruler to compare the measures. Write $<$, $>$, or $=$ in each ◯.

7. $4\frac{3}{16}$ in. ◯ $3\frac{15}{16}$ in.

8. $3\frac{6}{8}$ in. ◯ $3\frac{3}{4}$ in.

9. $2\frac{3}{8}$ in. ◯ $2\frac{3}{16}$ in.

Mixed Applications

10. Karina's art teacher gave her an $8\frac{1}{2}$-inch by 11-inch piece of paper. He told her to leave a $\frac{3}{4}$-inch margin on all 4 sides. What are the dimensions of the remaining area?

_____

11. Eliza measures her hair ribbon. It is $9\frac{10}{16}$ inch long. Mindy's hair ribbon is $9\frac{5}{8}$ inch long. Who has the longer hair ribbon?

_____

Changing Customary Units

Write *multiply* or *divide* to tell how to change the unit.

1. feet to inches _____

2. miles to yards _____

3. feet to yards _____

4. feet to miles _____

Change the unit. You may use a calculator.

5. 3 ft   = _____ in.

6. 4 yd   = _____ ft

7. 60 in. = _____ ft

8. 3 yd   = _____ in.

9. 36 ft = _____ yd

10. 1,760 yd = _____ mi

Write *more* or *fewer*.

11. When I change yards to feet, I expect to have _____ feet.

12. When I change yards to miles, I expect to have _____ miles.

Write *multiply* or *divide*. Solve.

13. How many yards are in 2 miles?

14. How many yards are in 126 feet?

_____

_____

Mixed Applications

For Problems 15–17, use the diagram at the right.

15. Mr. Rogers is decorating his classroom for a year-end party. He is measuring the width of his room. How many feet is the width?

_____

Mr. Rogers's Classroom

$w = 192$ in.

$l = 312$ in.

16. Mr. Rogers plans to hang crepe paper across the front of the classroom. Should he buy the 5-foot, 15-foot, or 30-foot length?

17. In feet, what are the area and perimeter of Mr. Rogers's classroom?

_____

_____

_____

Computing Customary Units

Rename the measurements.

1. 45 in.　　= _____ ft _____ in.

2. 14 ft　　= _____ yd _____ ft

3. 8 ft 19 in. = 9 ft _____ in.

4. 3 ft 3 in.　= 2 ft _____ in.

5. 9 yd 2 ft　= 8 yd _____ ft

6. 13 yd 4 ft = 14 yd _____ ft

Find the sum or difference.

7.　　6 ft　5 in.
　　+3 ft　9 in.
　　_____

8.　　8 ft　10 in.
　　+2 ft　　7 in.
　　_____

9.　　3 yd　2 ft
　　+4 yd　2 ft
　　_____

10.　　7 ft　3 in.
　　−3 ft　6 in.
　　_____

11.　　9 yd　7 ft
　　−6 yd　8 ft
　　_____

12.　　12 ft　　4 in.
　　− 6 ft　11 in.
　　_____

Mixed Applications

13. Cobb buys $2\frac{1}{2}$ yards of striped fabric and $3\frac{1}{3}$ yards of printed fabric. How much fabric does Cobb buy in all?

14. Dolores is counting the change in her drawer. When she gets 6 more nickels, she will have $5 in nickels. How many nickels does she have now?

15. Nasira is buying ribbon to frame the perimeter of a wall hanging that is 50 inches long and 60 inches wide. If ribbon is sold by the yard, how many yards does she need?

16. Masha and Lu are cutting pieces of rope. Masha cuts 4 feet 5 inches of rope. Lu cuts 3 feet 17 inches of rope. Who has the larger piece of rope?

Capacity

Change the unit.

1. 16 pt = _____ gal

2. 10 c = _____ pt

3. 4 qt = _____ c

4. 1 gal = _____ c

5. 32 fl oz = _____ pt

6. 4 qt = _____ pt

7. 16 qt = _____ gal

8. 8 c = _____ fl oz

For Exercises 9–12, use the picture.

9. How many pints of ice cream?

_____

ICE CREAM $\frac{1}{2}$ gal   SODA 8 fl oz   COTTAGE CHEESE 16 fl oz   SYRUP 24 fl oz

10. How many cups of soda?

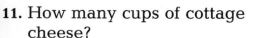
_____

11. How many cups of cottage cheese?

_____

12. How many pints of syrup?

_____

Write <, >, or = in each ◯.

13. 3 gal ◯ 14 qt

14. 1 qt ◯ 32 fl oz

15. 5 c ◯ 32 fl oz

16. 132 fl oz ◯ 1 gal

17. 5 qt ◯ 20 c

18. 8 pt ◯ 3 qt

Mixed Applications

19. The water cooler in Juan-Carlos's office uses 5-gallon bottles of water. How many cups can each bottle fill?

_____

20. Sharon is bringing orange juice to the class party. She needs enough juice to fill 24 cups. How many quarts of juice should she buy?

_____

Weight

What unit would you use to describe the weight of these objects? Write *tons*, *pounds*, or *ounces*.

1. a 20-inch TV

_____

2. a hamburger

_____

3. a 747 airplane

_____

Write *more* or *fewer* for each statement.

4. When I change tons to ounces, I expect to have

_____ ounces.

5. When I change ounces to pounds, I expect to have

_____ pounds.

Write *multiply* or *divide.* Change the unit. You may use a calculator.

6. 30 lb = __?__ oz

_____

7. 32,000 oz = __?__ T

_____

8. 3 T = __?__ lb

_____

Write which one is heavier.

9. 40 oz or 2 lb

_____

10. 3,000 lb or 2 T

_____

11. $\frac{1}{2}$ T or 1,500 lb

_____

Mixed Applications

12. At Wally's, a 12-ounce box of sunflower seeds sells for $2.59. At Barney's, sunflower seeds sell for $3.14 per pound. Which is the better buy?

_____

13. Fred has 36 feet of fencing to build a pen for his pet duck. What dimensions should he make the pen to get the greatest possible area?

_____

Name _____

Elapsed Time

Write the elapsed time for each hike.

1.

Time the   Time the
hike started   hike finished

Elapsed time _____

2.

Time the   Time the
hike started   hike finished

Elapsed time _____

Look at Nadeem's schedule for the day and complete the table.

	Activity	Starting Time	Ending Time	Elapsed Time
3.	School	8:05 A.M.	2:25 P.M.	_____
4.	Baseball practice	2:45 P.M.	_____	2 hr 35 min
5.	Dinner	_____	6:34 P.M.	31 min
6.	Homework	6:38 P.M.	7:57 P.M.	_____

Mixed Applications

For Problems 7–8, use the calendars.

7. Mr. Scopa's fifth-grade class is going on a 60-hour class trip. If they leave at 9 A.M. on June 3, when do they return?

_____

8. An 8-week weekday summer camp begins on June 24. What is the final day of camp?

_____

9. Julie bought 16 pounds of apples at $1.69 per pound. How much did Julie pay?

_____

JUNE						
Sun	Mon	Tue	Wed	Thu	Fri	Sat
						1
2	3	4	5	6	7	8
9	10	11	12	13	14	15
16	17	18	19	20	21	22
23 30	24	25	26	27	28	29

JULY						
Sun	Mon	Tue	Wed	Thu	Fri	Sat
	1	2	3	4	5	6
7	8	9	10	11	12	13
14	15	16	17	18	19	20
21	22	23	24	25	26	27
28	29	30	31			

AUGUST						
Sun	Mon	Tue	Wed	Thu	Fri	Sat
				1	2	3
4	5	6	7	8	9	10
11	12	13	14	15	16	17
18	19	20	21	22	23	24
25	26	27	28	29	30	31

Problem-Solving Strategy

Make a Table

Make a table to solve.

1. The pool at the community center is used from 6:00 A.M. until 8:30 A.M. by the swim team. Then there is a one-hour open swim followed by four 45-minute swim classes. At what time is the pool available again?

2. Tomás arrives at camp at 9:30 A.M. He has swimming for $1\frac{1}{2}$ hours, archery for 1 hour, and lunch for 30 minutes. Then he has crafts for $2\frac{1}{2}$ hours. At what time does Tomás finish crafts?

3. The youth symphony begins auditions at 10:00 A.M. Each student is given 10 minutes to perform. If Claudia is the 12th in line, at what time is her audition?

4. Kelly reads stories to children at the library. There are 3 sessions. Each lasts 45 minutes, with 30 minutes between sessions. If Kelly starts reading at 10:00 A.M., at what time does she finish?

Mixed Applications

Solve.

CHOOSE A STRATEGY

- Work Backward • Make a Table • Guess and Check • Write a Number Sentence

5. It is now 6:30 P.M. Jerry has just finished eating dinner, which took 40 minutes. Before that, he was at soccer practice for 2 hours and 45 minutes. At what time did soccer practice begin?

6. Holly exercises for 20 minutes a day for 3 weeks. Then she exercises for 30 minutes a day for 2 weeks. At the end of the fifth week, how many hours has Holly exercised?

7. Yoma bought a 35-ounce box of raisins for $3.79. Gloria paid $1.79 for a pound of raisins. Who got the better bargain?

8. Gil's mom changes the oil in her car every 3,000 miles. If she drives 18,000 miles per year, how many times does she change her oil each year?

Name _____

Temperature Changes

Vocabulary

Fill in the blanks.

1. _____ _____ are customary
   units for measuring temperature.

2. _____ _____ are metric units
   for measuring temperature.

Find the difference in temperature.

3. the temperature of the oven,
   78°C, and the temperature of
   the room, 20°C

   _____

4. the temperature at the indoor
   pool, 85°F, and the temperature
   outside, 37°F

   _____

5. the temperature at the mountain-
   top, ⁻6°F, and the temperature at
   the base, 37°F

   _____

6. the temperature in the freezer,
   ⁻12°C, and the temperature in
   the room, 23°C

   _____

Complete the table.

	Starting Temperature	Change in Temperature	Final Temperature
7.	6°C	rose 23°C	_____
8.	73°F	_____	27°F
9.	_____	fell 26°C	⁻3°C
10.	58°F	_____	75°F

Mixed Applications

11. At dusk the temperature was 37°F.
    The temperature had fallen 15°F
    by sunrise. At noon the tempera-
    ture was 28°F warmer. What was
    the temperature at noon?

    _____

12. Lucas bikes $3\frac{1}{2}$ miles on the
    bike trail. Ben bikes $2\frac{3}{8}$ miles.
    How much farther does Lucas
    bike than Ben?

    _____

Multiplying Fractions and Whole Numbers

Write a number sentence for each picture.

1.

2.

3.

4.

_____ _____ _____ _____

5.

6.

7.

8.

_____ _____ _____ _____

9.

10.

_____ _____

Find the product.

11. $\frac{1}{6} \times 18 =$ _____

12. $\frac{1}{7} \times 21 =$ _____

13. $\frac{1}{4} \times 16 =$ _____

14. $\frac{3}{8} \times 24 =$ _____

15. $\frac{2}{7} \times 14 =$ _____

16. $\frac{5}{8} \times 24 =$ _____

17. $12 \times \frac{3}{4} =$ _____

18. $24 \times \frac{5}{6} =$ _____

19. $18 \times \frac{7}{9} =$ _____

Mixed Applications

20. Kimberly has 20 books. Of those books, $\frac{2}{5}$ are mysteries. How many books are mysteries?

21. Dan walks to the store every week. It is $\frac{11}{12}$ mile from his house. If he has walked $\frac{3}{4}$ mile, how far must he still walk?

_____ _____

Multiplying a Fraction by a Fraction

Make a paper-folding model to find the product.

1. $\frac{1}{3} \times \frac{1}{2} = n$ **2.** $\frac{1}{4} \times \frac{1}{5} = n$ **3.** $\frac{1}{4} \times \frac{3}{4} = n$

_____   _____   _____

Find the amount needed of each ingredient to cut the recipe in half.

Waffles		
2 eggs	$\frac{1}{2}$ teaspoon baking soda	$\frac{3}{4}$ cup milk
$\frac{7}{8}$ cup flour	$\frac{1}{4}$ teaspoon salt	$\frac{2}{3}$ cup butter
2 teaspoons baking powder	2 tablespoons sugar	$\frac{1}{2}$ teaspoon vanilla
	$\frac{3}{4}$ cup sour cream	

4. eggs   **5.** flour   **6.** baking powder   **7.** baking soda

_____   _____   _____   _____

8. salt   **9.** sugar   **10.** sour cream   **11.** milk

_____   _____   _____   _____

12. butter   **13.** vanilla

_____   _____

Mixed Applications

14. Mary spent $\frac{8}{9}$ hour working on homework. She spent $\frac{1}{4}$ of that time on science. What part of an hour did she spend on science?

15. Bob combined $\frac{1}{3}$ gallon of orange juice, $\frac{3}{4}$ gallon of pineapple juice, and $\frac{5}{12}$ gallon of ginger ale to make punch. How many gallons did he make?

_____   _____

More About Multiplying a Fraction by a Fraction

Write a number sentence for the picture.

1.

2.

3.

_____   _____   _____

Draw fraction squares to find the product.

4. $\frac{1}{3} \times \frac{1}{5} = n$ 5. $\frac{2}{5} \times \frac{1}{4} = n$ 6. $\frac{2}{3} \times \frac{1}{2} = n$ 7. $\frac{5}{6} \times \frac{2}{3} = n$

_____   _____   _____   _____

Multiply. Write the answer in simplest form.

8. $\frac{1}{6} \times \frac{1}{3} = n$ 9. $\frac{2}{3} \times \frac{3}{5} = n$ 10. $\frac{1}{4} \times \frac{2}{7} = n$ 11. $\frac{4}{5} \times \frac{3}{8} = n$

_____   _____   _____   _____

12. $\frac{1}{6} \times \frac{7}{8} = n$ 13. $\frac{3}{7} \times \frac{5}{8} = n$ 14. $\frac{11}{12} \times \frac{4}{9} = n$ 15. $\frac{7}{9} \times \frac{5}{6} = n$

_____   _____   _____   _____

Mixed Applications

16. Sarah found $\frac{15}{16}$ cup of sugar in the cupboard. She used $\frac{2}{3}$ cup to make cookies. How much sugar was left?

17. Tim has 3 cups of cream. His recipe calls for 36 fluid ounces of cream. How much cream is left after Tim makes the recipe?

_____   _____

Multiplying Fractions and Mixed Numbers

Write a number sentence for the picture.

1.

2.

3.

_____   _____   _____

Draw fraction squares to help you find the product.

4. $\frac{2}{5} \times 1\frac{1}{3} = n$

5. $\frac{2}{3} \times 2\frac{1}{4} = n$

6. $\frac{3}{4} \times 3\frac{2}{3} = n$

_____   _____   _____

Multiply. Write the answer in simplest form.

7. $\frac{1}{3} \times 2\frac{1}{4} = n$

8. $\frac{1}{6} \times 3\frac{1}{2} = n$

9. $\frac{2}{3} \times 1\frac{1}{2} = n$

_____   _____   _____

10. $\frac{5}{6} \times 1\frac{2}{3} = n$

11. $\frac{3}{4} \times 2\frac{4}{5} = n$

12. $\frac{1}{3} \times 3\frac{2}{5} = n$

_____   _____   _____

13. $\frac{2}{3} \times 2\frac{2}{3} = n$

14. $\frac{1}{2} \times 3\frac{5}{6} = n$

15. $\frac{3}{5} \times 1\frac{3}{4} = n$

_____   _____   _____

Mixed Applications

16. On a recent trip, Mosi drove $2\frac{1}{2}$ hours on Monday, $1\frac{5}{6}$ hours on Tuesday, and $2\frac{2}{3}$ hours on Wednesday. How many hours did Mosi drive in all?

17. Martha had $3\frac{1}{3}$ dozen eggs. She used $\frac{3}{4}$ dozen to make cookies for a bake sale. How many dozen eggs does she have left?

Name _____

Problem-Solving Strategy

Make a Model

Make a model to solve.

1. Casey has $3\frac{1}{5}$ yards of white yarn. Of that, $\frac{3}{4}$ is wool. How many yards of white wool yarn does Casey have?

_____

2. Sam is taller than Brian. Betty is shorter than Sam, but taller than Susan. Susan is taller than Brian. Who is the shortest person?

_____

3. A garden has an area of $12\frac{3}{4}$ square yards. Roses cover $\frac{1}{3}$ of the garden, and sunflowers cover $\frac{1}{4}$ of the garden. How many square yards do the roses cover? the sunflowers?

_____

_____

4. Toby found $2.29 in coins. Of those coins, 5 are quarters. He has four times as many nickels as quarters. The rest are pennies. How many of each coin does he have?

_____

_____

Mixed Applications

Solve.

┌─────────────────────────┐
│ **CHOOSE A STRATEGY** │
└─────────────────────────┘

• Find a Pattern   • Write a Number Sentence   • Guess and Check   • Work Backward   • Make a Model

5. Ann and Bob went to a movie. Together they had $27.60. The tickets cost $6.50 each. Each bought a drink for $2.30 and a small popcorn for $1.75. Movie trading cards cost $0.65 a pack. How many packs of trading cards could they buy?

_____

6. A bus picks up 1 person at the first stop, 3 people at the second stop, 7 at the third stop, and 13 at the fourth stop. If this pattern continues, how many people will get on at the fifth stop? the sixth stop?

_____

Line Relationships

Vocabulary

Write the correct letter from Column 2.

Column 1

_____ 1. lines in a plane that never intersect and are the same distance from each other

_____ 2. lines that intersect to form four right angles

_____ 3. a flat surface with no end

_____ 4. a part of a line

_____ 5. lines that cross at one point

Column 2

a. perpendicular

b. plane

c. line segment

d. parallel

e. intersecting

For Exercises 6–9, use the figure.

6. Name the point where $\overline{AC}$ and $\overline{DC}$ intersect.

_____

7. Name a line segment on plane $ABCD$ that is

perpendicular to $\overline{AB}$. _____

8. Name a line segment that intersects but is

not perpendicular to $\overline{AB}$. _____

9. Name the line segment that is parallel to $\overline{AB}$.

_____

Mixed Applications

10. In Carvertown, Main Street and James Street are perpendicular. What kind of angles are formed at their intersection?

_____

11. Ben must drive 270 miles on Highway 5. He has now driven $\frac{1}{3}$ of the way. How many miles has he driven?

_____

Rays and Angles

Vocabulary

Complete.

1. A _____ is part of a line that has one endpoint and goes on forever in one direction.

2. An _____ is formed when two rays have the same endpoint.

Identify the angle. Write *right*, *acute*, or *obtuse*.

3.

4.

5.

6.

_____ _____ _____ _____

For Exercises 7–15, use the figure. Identify the angle. Write right, acute, or obtuse.

7. ∠AGB

8. ∠CGB

9. ∠FGA

_____ _____ _____

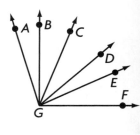

10. ∠AGF

11. ∠FGB

12. ∠EGF

_____ _____ _____

13. ∠BGF

14. ∠EGB

15. ∠DGB

_____ _____ _____

Mixed Applications

16. Luis is following a trail. If the points on the trail were labeled as shown, describe ∠BCD.

_____

17. The trail is 35 miles long. Luis has hiked 7 miles. What fraction of the trail has he hiked?

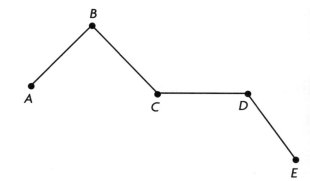

_____

Name _____

Measuring Angles

Vocabulary

Complete.

1. The unit used to measure an angle is called a _____ .

2. A _____ is a tool for measuring the size of the opening of an angle.

Use a protractor to measure each angle.

3.

_____

4.

_____

5.

_____

6.

_____

7.

_____

8.

_____

Mixed Applications

For Problems 9–10, use the road map.

9. What is the measure of the angle formed by the roads with Otan as the vertex?

_____

10. Sara went from Tolap to Milan to Otan and back to Tolap. How many miles did she travel?

_____

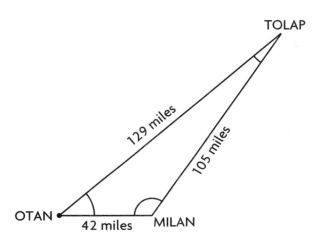

Problem-Solving Strategy

Draw a Diagram

Draw a diagram and solve.

1. Chad is planning to meet Sara at the Fruit Market. Sara gives Chad the directions to the Fruit Market. Make a map from Sara's directions.

O	Ride your bike south onto
	Highway 17 for 5 miles. Make a
	90° turn west on Highway 60.
	Ride 2 miles. Make a 90° turn
O	south on Highway 11 and ride
	1 mile. Look for the Fruit Market
	on your right.

2. Henry is helping his father nail down a new roof. He puts a nail every 4 inches along one edge of the roof. He puts a nail at each end. The roof is 10 feet long. How many nails does Henry use?

3. Sam is decorating a cake. He plans to put a candy rose every inch around the edge. The cake is 20 inches around the edge. How many candy roses does he need?

Mixed Applications

Solve.

CHOOSE A STRATEGY

• **Write a Number Sentence** • **Use a Schedule** • **Make a Model** • **Draw a Diagram**

4. On the way to the mountains, John, Mary, and Sue all rode in the back seat. John does not like to sit by a window. Mary does not like to sit behind the driver. From left to right, who sat where?

5. Fred bought some nails to build a bookcase. He bought $\frac{1}{4}$ pound of 1-inch nails, $\frac{1}{2}$ pound of $1\frac{1}{2}$-inch nails, and $\frac{1}{8}$ pound of 2-inch nails. How many pounds of nails did he buy?

6. Laura has $2.80 in change. She has pennies, nickels, and dimes. She has 6 nickels and 4 times as many dimes as nickels. How many pennies does she have?

7. Jan builds a rectangular fence 12 ft long and 8 ft wide. She places a post every 4 ft. How many posts does Jan need?

Classifying Quadrilaterals

Vocabulary

Write the correct letter from Column 2.

Column 1   **Column 2**

_____ 1. has 4 congruent sides and 2 pairs of
      congruent angles   **a.** quadrilateral

_____ 2. has 2 pairs of congruent sides and 2 pairs of   **b.** trapezoid
      parallel sides
                                                          c. parallelogram

_____ 3. has 4 sides of any length and 4 angles of   **d.** rhombus
      any size

_____ 4. has only 1 pair of parallel sides

Draw and name the quadrilateral.

5. adjacent sides not equal; 2 pairs   **6.** opposite sides not parallel;
of congruent sides; 4 right angles   4 sides and 4 angles

_____   _____

For Problems 7–10, write *true* or *false.*

7. A trapezoid has 4 right angles.   **8.** A square has 4 congruent sides.

_____   _____

9. A rectangle has 2 pairs of   **10.** A trapezoid has only one pair of
parallel sides.   parallel sides.

_____   _____

11. Dolores walked the perimeter of   **12.** Tom rode his bike for 3 hours
a park. It was 110 feet on all   every day after school for a
sides. Each corner was a 90°   week. His speed was 6 mph.
angle. What shape was the park?   How many miles did Tom ride
                                          his bike?

_____   _____

Classifying Triangles

Vocabulary

Complete.

1. A triangle in which each side is a different length is _____.

2. A triangle that has 2 congruent sides is _____.

Name each triangle. Write *isosceles, scalene,* or *equilateral.*

3.
3 in. 4 in. 6 in.

_____

4.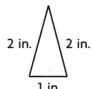
2 in. 2 in. 1 in.

_____

5.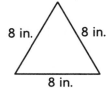
8 in. 8 in. 8 in.

_____

6.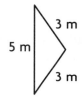
3 m 5 m 3 m

_____

7.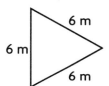
6 m 6 m 6 m

_____

8.
6 m 2 m 5 m

_____

Measure the sides. Classify each triangle. Write *isosceles, scalene,* or *equilateral.*

9.

_____

10.

_____

11.

_____

Mixed Applications

12. Julie wants to draw a triangle. She knows that one angle is 70° and another is 55°. How many degrees should the third angle be? How would you classify the triangle?

_____

13. Larry was on a trip with his father. They drove for 4 hours at 60 mph. After lunch they drove $3\frac{1}{2}$ hours at 40 mph. How far did they drive in all?

_____

More About Classifying Triangles

Vocabulary

Write the correct letter from Column 2.

Column 1	Column 2
_____ 1. a triangle that has one obtuse angle	**a.** right triangle
_____ 2. a triangle that has three acute angles	**b.** acute triangle
_____ 3. a triangle that has a right angle	**c.** obtuse triangle

Name each triangle. Write *right*, *acute*, or *obtuse*.

4.

5.

6.

_____

_____

_____

Find the measure of the unknown angle in each triangle.

7.

60°
50°
?

8.

15°
90°
?

9.
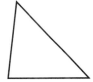
?
40°   40°

_____

_____

_____

Mixed Applications

10. Kyle cut a rectangular-shaped cake in half by cutting it from corner to corner. He made two triangular-shaped cakes. How would you classify the triangles he formed?

_____

11. Patty started her test at 8:30. She finished the test in 1 hour 20 minutes. Then she spent 1 hour 35 minutes in the library. At what time was she done?

_____

Name _____

Testing for Congruence

Use a ruler and a protractor to test each pair of figures for congruency. Write *congruent* or *not congruent*.

1.

_____

2.

_____

3.

_____

Write the letters of the two figures that are congruent.

4. a.

b.

c.

5. a.

b.

c.

_____

Mixed Applications

For Problem 6, use the drawing.

6. Grace and Harry are building birdhouses to raise money for charity. Including the end, side, and bottom that are not seen, they use 5 pieces of wood and a round dowel. Name the pieces that are congruent.

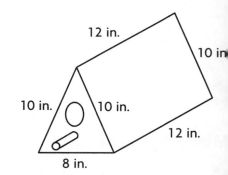

_____

7. They plan to sell birdhouses for $8.50 each. It costs $1.45 for materials to make one. If they sell 10 birdhouses how much money will they make?

_____

Congruence and Symmetry

Tell whether the two halves of each drawing are congruent.
Write *yes* or *no*.

1.

2.

3.

_____   _____   _____

Draw the lines of symmetry for each figure.

4.

5.

6.

7.

8.

9.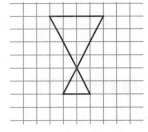

Mixed Applications

For Problems 10–11, use the letters.

10. Which letter has both point and
line symmetry?

H O T

_____

11. Which letter has exactly two lines
of symmetry?

12. Find the change from a $20 bill
for purchases totalling $17.21.

_____   _____

Transformations on the Coordinate Grid

Vocabulary

Complete.

1. When you move a figure to show a translation, reflection,

   or rotation, it is called a _____ .

Translate, reflect, and rotate each figure on the coordinate grid. Draw the new figure with its coordinates. Name the new ordered pairs.

2.

3.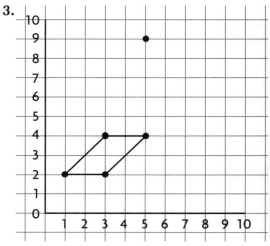

Mixed Applications

4. Sid wants to move his doghouse from its location at (2,3), (4,3), (2,6), and (4,6). The new ordered pairs for the location are (5,1), (5,3), (8,1), and (8,3). Use a coordinate grid to draw the figure representing the doghouse in its new location. Explain how the doghouse was moved.

   _____

   _____

   _____

5. Wesley started walking at 9:30 A.M. He took a 45-minute break for lunch and two 10-minute breaks to rest. He finished his walk at 4:50 P.M. How long was Wesley walking?

   _____

Tessellations

Vocabulary

Complete.

1. When closed figures are arranged to cover a surface with no

   gaps and no overlaps, it is called a _____.

Trace and cut out each figure. Write *yes* or *no* to tell whether each figure tessellates.

2.

_____

3.

_____

4.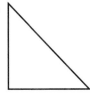

_____

Trace and cut out each figure. Translate, reflect, or rotate it to make a design that tessellates.

5.

6.

7.

8.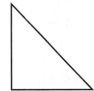

Mixed Applications

9. Shirley is buying 12-inch-square tiles for $1.55 each. She wants to cover her bathroom floor. It is 9 ft long and 9 ft wide. How many tiles will she need? What will they cost?

_____

10. Dennis is using hexagonal and triangular tiles to cover his wall. Draw the design that Dennis will have on his wall.

Name _____

Problem-Solving Strategy

Make a Model

Make a model to solve.

1. Fred is making a tabletop with a mosaic design. He can use two or more polygons. The polygons need to tessellate to cover the tabletop. Use pattern blocks to make a design that tessellates. Draw your design.

2. Art has pattern blocks that are a small equilateral triangle, small square, and small parallelogram. Which two of these blocks will tessellate when arranged in a design? Draw the design.

3. Betty wanted to budget her free time on weekends. She planned to spend $\frac{1}{2}$ of her time on chores, $\frac{1}{3}$ of her time playing with friends, and $\frac{1}{6}$ of her time reading. She read for 2 hours. How many hours did she play with her friends?

4. Tony makes picture frames from wood molding to sell at the craft fair. He has 40 inches of molding. He wants to create the largest possible picture frame. What dimensions should the frame be to give the greatest possible area?

Mixed Applications

Solve.

CHOOSE A STRATEGY

• Make a Graph • Write a Number Sentence • Work Backward • Make a Model • Draw a Diagram

5. Marcus is making a design using hexagons. Above each hexagon, he wants to put two trapezoids. His design calls for 215 hexagons. How many trapezoids will he need for his design?

6. Jane wants to tile her 8 ft by 10 ft dining area and her 12 ft by 12 ft kitchen with the same tile. How many square feet does she have to cover?

Construct a Circle

Vocabulary

Write the correct letter from Column 2.

Column 1

Column 2

1. chord _____

a. A tool for constructing circles

2. diameter _____

b. A line segment that connects the center with a point on the circle

3. circle _____

c. A line segment that connects any two points on the circle

4. radius _____

d. A closed figure with all points on the figure the same distance from the center point. It has no beginning point and no ending point.

5. compass _____

e. A chord that passes through the center of the circle

Use a compass to construct the circle and find the measurements.

6. Construct a circle with a radius of 2 cm. Label and measure a diameter, radius, and chord.

Write *chord, diameter,* or *radius* for each line segment.

7.

_____

8.

_____

9.

_____

Mixed Applications

10. Josephine knows that the diameters of the two hoops are 20 in. and 18 in. What is the radius of each hoop?

_____

11. Alice was in the library from 3:30 to 5:45 each afternoon after school this week. How long did she spend in the library?

_____

Finding Circumference

Vocabulary

Fill in the blank.

1. The perimeter of a circle is the _____.

---

2. Use a ruler and string to find the circumference of a pencil or crayon.

Use a calculator to divide the circumference of each object by its diameter. Complete the table.

Object	Circumference (c)	Diameter (d)	$\frac{c}{d}$
3. Plate	12.6 in.	4 in.	_____
4. Tire	125.6 in.	40 in.	_____
5. Jar	15.7 in.	5 in.	_____

Mixed Applications

For Problems 6–7, use the pictures.

6. What is the perimeter of the smallest box that this record can fit into?

_____

8 in.

7. What is the radius of the record?

_____

8. A record costs $4.99. Joe wants to buy one for himself and one for each of his 5 friends. How much would it cost Joe for the records?

_____

9. Florence has 56 stickers. She wants to give 4 friends her stickers. How many stickers will each friend get?

_____

Problem-Solving Strategy

Act It Out

Act it out to solve. Round to the nearest tenth when necessary.

1. Sylvia is making a flower vase. She wants to cover the cylindrical part of the vase with tissue paper. The cylinder is 18 cm in height, and its diameter is 7 cm. What is the circumference of the cylinder? What size should Sylvia cut the tissue paper to fit the cylinder exactly?

_____

_____

2. Robert made a cylinder out of clay. He wants to cover it with a piece of newspaper. The cylinder is 14 in. high and has a diameter of 5 in. The piece of newspaper he has is 18 in. by 16 in. Does Robert have enough paper? Explain.

_____

_____

3. Melanie bought a book for $12.75. She handed the clerk a $20 bill. What combination of bills and coins could she get back as her change?

_____

_____

4. Tyler had two $5 bills, two $10 bills, one $20 bill, one $1 bill, 2 quarters, 2 dimes, 1 nickel, and 4 pennies. He spent $12.00. He put $29.41 in the bank. What bills and coins does Tyler have left?

_____

_____

Mixed Applications

Solve.

┌─── CHOOSE A STRATEGY ───┐

• Work Backward   • Make a Model   • Draw a Diagram   • Act It Out   • Write a Number Sentence

5. Fiona needs to wrap a cylindrical box. It is 14 in. in height, and its diameter is 8 in. What is the circumference of the cylinder? What size paper will Fiona need?

_____

6. Derek, Rose, Juan, Laura, and Jeff are in line at the snack counter. Jeff is in front of Rose and after Derek. Juan is between Laura and Derek. Who is last in line?

_____

Angles in a Circle

Write *true* or *false* to describe each statement.

1. There are four 90° angles in a circle.

_____

2. There are 361° in a circle.

_____

3. You can divide a right angle into two acute angles.

_____

4. If six of seven angles in a circle measure 55°, the seventh angle measures 55° too.

_____

Find the missing angle.

5.

_____

6.

_____

7.

_____

8.

_____

Mixed Applications

For Problem 9, use the clocks.

9. Which clock shows an obtuse angle?

_____

Clock A

Clock B

10. Toni has a jar she wants to decorate with felt. The jar is 15 cm high. Its diameter is 10 cm. What is the circumference of the jar? What size felt will Toni need?

_____

11. Jon has 4 tickets to a soccer game. If each ticket costs $5.95, how much did Jon spend on tickets?

_____

Name _____

LESSON
25.4

Measuring Angles in a Circle

Use a protractor to find the number of degrees in the angles of the circle.

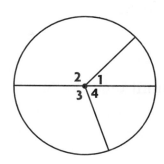

1. How many degrees are in angle 4?

_____

2. How many degrees are in angle 3?

_____

3. How many degrees are in angle 1?

_____

4. How many degrees are in angle 2?

5. How many degrees are in angles 1, 2, 3, and 4 in all?

_____   _____

Use a compass and a protractor to draw a circle with the following angles.

6. 5 angles of 72° each   7. 4 angles of 90° each   8. 2 angles of 130° each and 2 angles of 50° each

Mixed Applications

9. The school bus will pick up students only within a 2-mile radius of the school. To get to Lisa's house from school, you drive 2 miles south, make a 90° turn and drive 2 miles west. Can Lisa ride the school bus? Why or why not?

_____

_____

10. Chad went to the store. He bought 2 T-shirts for $12 each, a pair of jeans for $25, and 3 pairs of shoes for $21 each. How much money did Chad spend in all?

_____

_____

ON MY OWN   P149

Prisms and Pyramids

Vocabulary

Fill in the blanks.

1. A _____ is a solid figure that has two

   congruent faces called _____.

2. A _____ is a solid figure with

   one _____ that is a polygon and three
   or more faces that are triangles with a common vertex.

Write *prism* or *pyramid*. Write the polygon that names the base. Identify the
solid figure.

3.

4.

5.

_____   _____   _____

_____   _____   _____

Write the name of the solid figure. Make a drawing of each.

6. I have 2 congruent pentagons for
   bases. I have 5 rectangular faces.

   _____

7. I have a base with 8 equal sides.
   My faces are 8 triangles.

   _____

Mixed Applications

8. Name two items that look like a
   cube.

   _____

   _____

9. Scott spent 18 hours driving to
   college. If his average speed was
   55 mph, how many miles did
   Scott drive?

   _____

Nets for Solid Figures

Vocabulary

Complete.

_____ is a two-dimensional pattern for a three-dimensional solid.

Match each solid figure with its net. Write *a, b, c,* or *d.*

1.

2.

3.

4.

_____ _____ _____ _____

a.

b.

c.

d.

Circle the letter of the pattern that can be folded to make the figure.

5.

a.

b.

c.

6.

a.

b.

c.

Mixed Applications

7. What faces would you find in a net for a square pyramid?

_____

_____

8. Cara earns $36.75 a week for 7 hours of babysitting. How much does she earn in 4 weeks? How much does she earn an hour?

_____

_____

Name _____

Solid Figures from Different Views

Use grid paper to draw each figure from the top, the side, and the front.

1.
2.
3.

Choose the figure that is represented by each set of three drawings.

From the top   From the side   From the front

4.

a.

5.

b.

6.

c.

Mixed Applications

7. Bricks are stacked in 8 rows with 6 blocks in each row. If 10 layers of bricks are stacked, how many are in the stack?

8. A survey of 90 drivers found that $\frac{5}{6}$ of the people had taken driving lessons. How many of the drivers took driving lessons?

lgebraic Thinking: Volume

nd the missing dimension. You may use a calculator.

1.

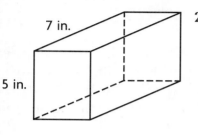

7 in.

5 in.

Volume = 140 cu in.

width = _____

2.

3 cm

4 cm

Volume = 108 cu cm

height = _____

3.

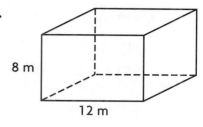

8 m

12 m

Volume = 672 cu m

length = _____

4. length = 11 yd

width = 5 yd

height = _____

Volume = 165 cu yd

5. length = 14 ft

width = 9 ft

height = 4 ft

Volume = _____

6. length = 8 in.

width = _____

height = 9 in.

Volume = 288 cu in.

omplete the table. You may use a calculator.

	Length	Width	Height	Volume
7.	15 in.	_____	2 in.	240 cu in.
8.	_____	11 m	5 m	385 cu m
9.	6 yd	8 yd	_____	288 cu yd
0.	5 cm	3 cm	15 cm	_____

ixed Applications

. A carton is 9 inches wide,
6 inches long, and 5 inches high.
What is the volume of the carton?

_____

12. Tom wants to buy a stereo that
costs $540. He has saved $\frac{1}{3}$ of the
cost. How much has Tom saved?

_____

Problem-Solving Strategy

Use a Formula

Use a formula and solve.

1. A garden that is 18 feet wide and 22 feet long needs to be fenced. Will 25 yards of fencing be enough? Explain.

2. The trailer of a lumber truck is 15 feet wide, 18 feet long, and 10 feet high. Is the truck large enough to carry 2,500 cubic feet of lumber?

3. Tim is packing a box that is 18 inches long and 12 inches wide and has a volume of 3,240 cubic inches. He wants to pack an object that is 9 inches long, 6 inches wide, and 16 inches high. Will the object fit in the box? Explain.

4. New flooring is being installed in the school foyer. The area is 15 feet wide and 33 feet long. How many square yards of flooring is needed? What is the perimeter of the foyer, measured in feet?

Mixed Applications

Solve.

CHOOSE A STRATEGY

- Draw a Diagram   - Make a Table   - Use a Formula

5. Classes at the high school begin at 7:45 A.M. Each class is 50 minutes long, and there is a 7-minute break after each class. At what time does the second class of the day end?

6. A swimming pool is 60 feet long and 30 feet wide. How many cubic feet of water will be needed to fill the pool to a depth of 8 feet?

Estimating Volume

Use the benchmarks at the right to name the more reasonable unit for measuring the volume of each box. Estimate the volume.

 1 cubic
centimeter
(cu cm)

1 cubic
decimeter
(cu dm)

1.

3 dm

2 dm

6 dm

2.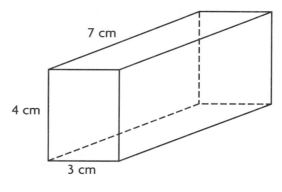

7 cm

4 cm

3 cm

_____

_____

_____

_____

Choose the most reasonable measure. Circle *a, b,* or *c.*

3. a desk   **a.** 25 cu in.   **b.** 25 cu ft   **c.** 25 cu yd

4. a breadbox   **a.** 360 cu in.   **b.** 360 cu ft   **c.** 360 cu yd

5. a barn   **a.** 480 cu in.   **b.** 480 cu ft   **c.** 480 cu yd

Mixed Applications

6. A carton is 12 inches long and 15 inches wide. Jon estimates the volume of the carton as 2,000 cubic inches. Ted says the estimated volume is 200 cubic inches. Which estimate is more reasonable?

7. A number is greater than 42 but less than 50. The sum of its digits is 11. What is the product of that number and 16?

_____

_____

Understanding Ratio

Vocabulary

Fill in the blank.

1. A _____ can be used to compare two numbers in three ways.

Name the type of ratio.

2. There were 4 baseballs and 6 basketballs.

_____

3. Margo had 3 quarters and 2 pennies.

_____

4. Recess is preferred by 19 of 20 students.

_____

5. Of 20 students, 11 are boys.

_____

Use the picture to make the comparison.

6.

_____ wings to _____ planes

7.

_____ flowers to _____ stem

8.

_____ legs to _____ spiders

9.

_____ fingers to _____ hands

Mixed Applications

10. Last month there were 21 days of school and 10 days off. What was the ratio of school days to total days?

_____

11. Mavis ran the 200-meter dash in 25.43 seconds. What does the digit 4 stand for?

_____

Name _____

Expressing Ratios

Write *a* or *b* to show which fraction represents the ratio.

1. 7 to 9 _____
   a. $\frac{9}{7}$ **b.** $\frac{7}{9}$

2. 6:2 _____
   a. $\frac{6}{2}$ **b.** $\frac{2}{6}$

3. 9:3 _____
   a. $\frac{9}{3}$ **b.** $\frac{3}{9}$

4. 11 to 16 _____
   a. $\frac{16}{11}$ **b.** $\frac{11}{16}$

For Exercises 5–7, use the table. Write each ratio in three ways.

5. What is the ratio of race games to sports games?

_____

6. What is the ratio of all games to arcade games?

_____

7. What is the ratio of sports games to all games?

_____

BEN'S VIDEOGAME COLLECTION	
Number of Games	Type
5	Race
3	Arcade
2	Sports

Mixed Applications

8. Becky took a survey of her classmates' pets. The students had 9 dogs and 13 cats. What was the ratio of cats to dogs?

_____

9. Kareem found that one-sixth of his jelly beans were red. If he had 84 jelly beans, what was the ratio of red jelly beans to the whole?

_____

10. Brian had a triangle with a 90° angle and a 19° angle. How many degrees were in the third angle?

_____

11. Erik discovered he was $\frac{3}{4}$ as tall as Wilt Chamberlain, the NBA legend. Chamberlain is 86 inches tall. How tall is Erik?

_____

Equivalent Ratios

Vocabulary

Fill in the blank.

1. _____ are ratios that
   show the same relationship.

Tell whether the ratios are equivalent. Write *yes* or *no*.

2. $\frac{3}{8}$ and $\frac{9}{24}$ _____

3. 4:5 and 5:4 _____

4. 7 to 4 and 28 to 16 _____

5. $\frac{8}{4}$ and $\frac{2}{1}$ _____

6. 6:8 and 2:4 _____

7. 3 to 15 and 4 to 20 _____

8. Complete the table.

Number of oranges to make orange juice	5	_____	_____	_____
Pints of orange juice	1	2	3	4

Write three ratios that are equivalent to the given ratio.

9. 7:1 _____

10. 6:3 _____

11. 3 to 2 _____

12. 13 to 15 _____

_____

_____

13. $\frac{5}{2}$ _____

14. $\frac{7}{8}$ _____

Mixed Applications

15. There are 35 campers at
    Backbush summer camp. Of
    those, 28 play baseball. What is
    the ratio of baseball players to
    all campers? Write the ratio in
    simplest form.

    _____

16. Katie is buying orange juice.
    She can buy 1 gallon for $2.75
    or 1 pint for $0.35. Which is the
    better buy?

    _____

More About Equivalent Ratios

Vocabulary

Fill in the blank.

1. A ratio that compares the distance on a map with the

   actual distance is a _____.

Copy and complete each ratio table.

2. Gallons of gas used	1	2	_____	7	_____
3. Miles traveled	18	36	90	_____	198

4. Number of minivans	1	4	7	_____	15
5. Number of passengers	7	28	_____	84	_____

For Problems 6–9, use the drawing of the patio.

6. What is the width of the pool in units?

   _____

7. What is the actual width of the pool?

   _____

pool

Scale:
1 linear unit = 4 ft

pool house

8. What is the perimeter of the pool house in units? in feet?

   _____

9. What is the ratio of linear units to feet?

   _____

10. A builder plans to use a scale of 2 cm = 5 ft in her plan for a house. What length will the lines be that represent 5 ft, 10 ft, 15 ft, 20 ft, and 25 ft?

    _____

11. A yard is 28 ft long and 36 ft wide. It costs $0.50 per square foot to have grass planted. What is the total cost?

    _____

Ratios in Similar Figures

Vocabulary

Fill in the blank.

1. In _____ figures, the matching angles are congruent and the sides have equivalent ratios.

Write *yes* or *no* to tell whether the shapes are similar.

2.

_____

3.

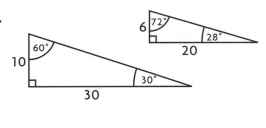

_____

Find the length of the missing side in the similar shapes.

4.

_____

5.

_____

6.

_____

7.

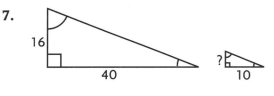

_____

Mixed Applications

8. A 10-pound slab of clay will make 15 12-inch flower pots. How many 6-inch flower pots will a slab of clay make?

_____

9. Karen makes payments of $199 per month for 3 years for her car. What is the total amount Karen pays for her car?

_____

Problem-Solving Strategy

Write a Number Sentence

Write a number sentence to solve.

1. Apu had a 3 in. × 5 in. photo that he wanted to enlarge. What is the width of the enlargement?

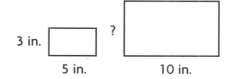

3 in.

5 in.   10 in.

?

_____

2. Joshua built a model plane that was $\frac{1}{25}$ the size of the actual plane. If the model was 2 feet long, how long was the actual plane?

3. Jane ran 1 mile south, 2 miles east, 1 mile north, and then returned to her starting point. How far did Jane run?

_____

Mixed Applications

Solve.

CHOOSE A STRATEGY

• Write a Number Sentence   • Draw a Diagram   • Act It Out   • Work Backward

4. Diana has a dining room table that is 8 feet long and 4 feet wide. She buys a tablecloth that is a similar rectangle and is 12 feet long. How wide is the tablecloth?

5. Majdeh bought a coat for $48.99, a scarf for $24.95, and a blouse for $19.95. She received $6.11 change. How much money did she give the cashier?

_____

6. Alfonse recorded the noon temperature for five days. On Monday and Thursday the temperature was 94°F. On Tuesday it was 78°F, on Wednesday it was 84°F, and on Friday it was 98°F. What was the mean temperature?

7. Yvette is painting her room. She has one wall left that is 9 ft × 14 ft. She has one quart of paint that covers 350 square feet. Will she be able to put two coats of paint on the wall?

_____

Understanding Percent

Vocabulary

Fill in the blank.

1. _____ means "per hundred."

Use counters to show the following on your 10 × 10 grids.
Draw a picture and write the percent.

2. 67 cents out of
   1 dollar

   _____

3. 16 sheep out of
   100 animals

   _____

4. 58 girls out of
   100 children

   _____

Look at the grid. Write the percent that is shaded.

5.

Percent _____

6.

Percent _____

7.

Percent _____

For Exercises 8–9, choose the more reasonable percent. Circle *a* or *b*.

8. "*About half* the students bring
   their own lunches to school,"
   said the cafeteria worker.

   a. 55 percent

   b. 85 percent

9. "*Very few* children are sent
   to the principal's office," said
   the teacher.

   a. 98 percent

   b. 2 percent

Mixed Applications

10. Lydia shot 100 free throws
    and made 84%. How many
    free throws did Lydia make?

    _____

11. Brian gave the cashier $1.00 for
    his fruit juice. He received $0.11
    in change. What percent of his
    dollar did he spend on the juice?

    _____

Connecting Percents and Decimals

For Exercises 1–4, study the shaded parts of the grid.

1. What percent of the squares have light shading? _____

2. What percent of the squares have dark shading? _____

3. Use the decimal form to add the light shading and no

   shading. _____

4. When you add the light shading, dark shading, and no shading,

   what percent is the total? _____

Write the number as a percent and as a decimal.

5. seventy-five hundredths

6. ninety-three hundredths

_____   _____

7. fifteen hundredths _____   8. thirty hundredths _____

Write the decimal as a percent.

9. 0.46 _____   10. 0.79 _____   11. 0.20 _____

12. 0.03 _____   13. 0.18 _____   14. 0.86 _____

Write the percent as a decimal.

15. 38% _____   16. 74% _____   17. 2% _____

18. 16% _____   19. 22% _____   20. 91% _____

Mixed Applications

For Problems 21–22, write the answer as a percent and as a decimal.

21. Sharon and Pete participated in a 100-mile fund-raising relay race. They ran a combined 23 miles. What part of the race did they cover?

22. Melanie received $100 for her birthday. She spent $38 on a new dress. What part did she spend on the dress?

_____   _____

Connecting Percents and Fractions

Write the percent as a fraction in simplest form.

1. 50% ————   2. 30% ————   3. 25% ————

4. fifty-six percent ————   5. twenty-three percent ————

Write the fraction as a percent.

6. $\frac{19}{100}$ ————   7. $\frac{8}{25}$ ————   8. $\frac{71}{100}$ ————

9. $\frac{2}{100}$ ————   10. $\frac{2}{10}$ ————   11. $\frac{1}{4}$ ————

Write as a decimal and as a fraction in simplest form.

12. 12 percent ————   13. 24 percent ————

14. 37 percent ————   15. 45 percent ————

16. 60 percent ————   17. 85 percent ————

18. 75 percent ————   19. 50 percent ————

Mixed Applications

20. Mr. Downing went on a 100-day archaeological expedition. He traveled $\frac{1}{5}$ of the days. What percent of the days did he not travel?

_____

21. Ken realized that it had been 100 days since school started. He counted 32 days off for holidays and weekends. What percent of days had school been in session?

_____

22. Brenda drank one-half gallon of milk a week. Linda drank 8 cups of milk a week. Who drank more milk? Explain.

_____

_____

23. The ratio of coaches to players is 1 to 12. There are 9 coaches. How many players are there?

_____

_____

Benchmark Percents

Vocabulary

Fill in the blank.

1. A _____ is a commonly used
   percent that is close to the amount you are estimating.

For Exercises 2–4, choose from the following benchmarks:
0%, 25%, 50%, 75%, and 100%.

2.

3.

4.

_____   _____   _____

Tell what benchmark percent you would use to estimate each percent.

5. 42% _____   6. 19% _____   7. 78% _____   8. 91% _____

For Exercises 9–10, choose the more reasonable benchmark
percent. Circle *a* or *b*.

9. *Most* of the class preferred recess
   to math.

   a. 75%

   b. 25%

10. *Very few* of the students failed
    the science exam.

    a. 40%

    b. 10%

Mixed Applications

11. Ben has finished reading nearly
    half of his book. What benchmark
    would you use to estimate the
    percent of the book he has read?

_____

12. Hasan earns $72 for 6 hours of
    work. How much does he earn
    for 4 hours of work? for 1 hour?

_____

Percents in Circle Graphs

For Exercises 1–2, use the first circle graph.

**STUDENTS WHO
HAVE PETS**

1. Do more than three quarters or less than three quarters of the students surveyed

   have pets? _____

2. What decimal represents students who

   have pets? _____

For Exercises 3–5, use the second circle graph.

TYPES OF PETS

3. Do more students have dogs or have other types of pets?

   _____

4. Which groups in the circle are the same size?

   _____

5. Which two categories cover less than one half of the circle graph?

   _____

Mixed Applications

For Exercises 6–10, use the table.

FAVORITE DESSERTS	
Ice cream	20 votes
Lemonade	10 votes
Cookies	20 votes

6. What decimal represents the students who chose ice cream? What percent of the students chose ice cream? (HINT: 20 out of 50 chose ice cream.)

   _____

7. What decimal and percent represent the students who chose lemonade?

   _____

8. What decimal and percent represent the students who chose cookies?

   _____

9. If you were to make a circle graph of these data, what would the smallest section show?

   _____

10. How many times as large would the section for ice cream be as the section for lemonade?

    _____

Problem-Solving Strategy

Make a Graph

Make a graph and solve.

1. Abigail surveyed the fifth-grade students to find out their favorite TV shows. She organized the data in the table at the right. What is the best way for her to display the data? Which TV show is most popular?

_____

_____

FAVORITE TV SHOWS	
Show	**Percent of Votes**
Plimpton	20%
Queen of the Hill	40%
Atlas	10%
Harborwatch	10%
The Butler	20%

Mixed Applications

Solve.

CHOOSE A STRATEGY

- **Make a Model**   • **Make a Graph**   • **Guess and Check**   • **Write a Number Sentence**

2. Tamala recorded the average temperature for 6 months. She recorded 48° in April, 59° in May, 69° in June, 76° in July, 74° in August, and 64° in September. Which month had the highest temperature? How can you show this?

_____

3. Mylan spent $3 on a magazine. He spent half of his remaining money on a video game. He then spent half of his remaining money on a book. He had $12 left. How much money did Mylan begin with?

_____

4. A dog pen will have a length of 18 feet and a width of 12 feet. One length will be formed by the side of a garage. The other three sides will be made of fencing. How much fencing is needed?

_____

5. There were 63 people in a hotel. Then 7 checked out, and 3 times that number checked in. How many people are in the hotel now?

_____